Second Edition

Placekicking Fundamentals and Techniques

Mastering the Mechanics of Placekicking and Exploiting the Scoring Potential of the Kicking Game

Steve Libassi

©2005 Coaches Choice. Second edition. All rights reserved. Printed in the United States. No part of this book may be reproduced, stored in a retrieval system, or transmitted, in any form or by any means, electronic, mechanical, photocopying, recording, or otherwise, without the prior permission of Coaches Choice.

ISBN: 1-58518-909-X
Library of Congress Control Number:2004112086
Cover design: Jeanne Hamilton
Cover photo: Tom Pidgeon/Getty Images
Book layout: Jeanne Hamilton

Coaches Choice
P.O. Box 1828
Monterey, CA 93942
www.coacheschoice.com

Dedication

To the Lord for all the gifts He continues to bestow upon me.

To my wife, Mary Sue, and sons, Nathan and Collin, for their belief in me, and their patient understanding during my long and frequent discourses on the kicking game at the dinner table.

And, finally, to David Crisafi, Shane Draper, Tom Hagan, and Daniel Payne. Your talent and work ethic will take you far.

Acknowledgments

John Moore inspired and pushed me to write this book, then provided invaluable content advice. John, I give you my most sincere appreciation for all your help and enthusiasm.

A big thank-you is also due the folks at Coaches Choice.

Contents

	Dedication	3
	Acknowledgements	4
	Introduction	6
Chapter 1:	Proper Form and Mechanics	7
Chapter 2:	Straight-On Placekicking	21
Chapter 3:	Soccer-Style Placekicking	29
Chapter 4:	Adjustments	44
Chapter 5:	Leg Flexibility and Strength	49
Chapter 6:	The Placekicking Team	66
Chapter 7:	Kickoffs	77
Chapter 8:	The Mental Side of Kicking	84
Chapter 9:	Equipment	87
Chapter 10:	Winning Practices, Game Preparation, and Games	94
	Epilogue	99
	About the Author	100

Introduction

"He's not a football player! He's just a kicker!"

"Aw, just kick the ball!"

"All you have to do is keep your head down and follow through."

"Wow, what a life! Come in two or three times a game and kick a field goal while all the other guys bust their tails all game long!"

"Why should I tie up valuable practice time and make a whole team stand around just to help one kid practice field goals when I'm not going to use him that much during the games?"

Sometimes I feel as if I have heard it all: the jokes, the ridicule, and the lack of appreciation for placekickers. It is a fact of life, though, that placekicking is not only under-coached and (maybe worse) mis-coached, but also the skill and training necessary to kick well is sorely underappreciated.

Placekicking may not be as physically demanding during the game, or as mentally challenging as other football positions, but, then, if it were that easy, wouldn't more players be doing it — at least as a sideline, while they play traditional positions? If placekicking were that easy, wouldn't there be more placekickers? Wouldn't competition for placekicking time be greater, especially at the college, high school, and recreational levels? Sure, and it is at these lower levels that good placekickers are most sorely needed and can have the greatest impact on a game's outcome.

Placekicking appears to be fairly basic: the placekicker lines up his kick, measures his steps, and kicks the ball through the goalposts. What could be simpler than that? But if you want to be a successful placekicker, or you want to groom a player to be a successful placekicker, and your goals are consistency as well as distance, then you will have to acknowledge that placekicking is more than just lining up and kicking the ball. The idea is not just to kick the ball; it is to kick the ball through the goalposts every time, regardless of the weather, field conditions, and distance — with only one try, with the team depending on you, with the fans for both teams screaming, with the defense yelling at you and taunting you and trying to block your kick, regardless of how good the snap and the hold are.

I competed as a placekicker for four years at the college level and as a 42-year-old backup Arena 2 placekicker, and I have coached college, high school, junior high school, and recreation league placekickers. On the basis of that experience, I can say with all confidence that, with proper training and the proper mind-set, an average athlete at these levels should be able to kick successfully 75 percent of the time up to 50, 45, 40, and 35 yards, respectively. That level of kicking can easily influence the outcome of a third of football games and, consequently, the success of a season.

1

Proper Form and Mechanics

Placekicking is no different from other sports skills in one important respect: proper form is essential. Leg strength and, to a lesser degree, how hard a placekicker kicks the ball will lead to distance, but not to accuracy. For example, a golfer must work to control his swing to generate the consistent accuracy and distance on which a respectable golf game is based. The harder a golfer swings, the less likely the golf ball will take the proper flight path to the desired spot because the club face is less likely to hit the ball the right way.

Another example is a baseball player trying to hit a home run; the harder he tries to hit it out of the park, the more likely he is to either miss the ball completely or to pop it up. However, when he maintains proper mechanics, swinging through the ball on the correct plane, his success rate increases dramatically, often with the feeling that he barely hit the ball. Again, it is not how much effort he expends; it is how well he maintains proper form and balance, and how well he strikes the ball.

In much the same way, the vast majority of a placekicker's accuracy and distance is determined by how well he prepares for the kick, approaches and makes contact with the ball, and follows through after contact. The distance being attempted magnifies the importance of proper form, since less margin for error exists the farther the kicker is from the goalposts.

(Note: While both the straight-on and soccer-style approaches will be discussed in depth during this and subsequent chapters, the reader should understand from the outset that the latter approach is much more difficult to coach and execute, even for the exceptional soccer player. Consequently, more coaching tips will be offered to help to ingrain in the placekicker the form necessary to successfully kick field goals using the soccer-style approach. For the reader's benefit, the discussion of the two approaches will be treated separately, with Chapter 2 devoted exclusively to the proper form and mechanics of the straight-on approach, and Chapter 3 devoted exclusively to the proper form and mechanics of the soccer-style approach. This chapter will discuss information pertinent to both approaches.)

Marking Off the Approach

Do not underrate the importance of marking off the steps properly, and never stop practicing it. Think about it. If the steps are not right, the kicking foot will not make proper contact with the ball. If the steps do not feel right after marking them off, re-mark them. Remember: a placekicker's number one objective is to always make contact with the ball at the same place with the same part of the foot. Thus, he must make sure to line up at the same distance and the same angle from the ball every time.

Whether working with a straight-on kicker or a soccer-style kicker, the one-and-a-half-step approach to the ball supplies all the momentum and power a placekicker will need to kick the ball more than 50 yards, without introducing the lack of control and balance that comes from a longer approach. Of course, the other benefit is that he will kick the ball in less time than he would with a two-and-a-half-step approach, making it harder for the field-goal blocking team to do its job.

Coaching Tip: As the placekicker's proficiency with the one-and-a-half-step approach (or any other length of approach, for that matter) improves, either he may need to move closer to the ball (to avoid topping the ball) or farther away (to avoid kicking "under" the ball). For example, if a placekicking student is having difficulty smoothing out his approach (consistently topping the ball so much that he kicks spirals through the goalposts), correct the problem by moving him eight inches closer to the ball, and then gradually moving him back to two inches as his one-and-half step approach improves and his stride to the ball lengthens.

The Approach

The first step of the approach is the most critical, and requires the greatest amount of work to master. It is a driving step, a large and aggressive step that acts in concert with the upper body, which is leaning into the ball, and the arms, which are thrusting forward to generate the necessary momentum and power. The initial drive step is not a hop step, nor is it a slide step.

Coaching Tip: One of the biggest problems many inexperienced placekickers have is learning how to execute the second step/hop. Emphasize to your placekicker that he must actually become airborne, that he must not drag his kicking leg along and swipe at the ball. Not only will he not be properly balanced, he will not have generated the necessary momentum (and subsequent power) into the kick. The cause of the problem is his preoccupation with kicking the ball, a preoccupation that causes him to focus solely on making solid contact with the ball. In other words, he is focusing too much on putting everything he has into the ball rather than preparing himself to deliver a balanced, powerful blow that can only be generated *consistently* by a proper approach. Have your kickers first concentrate on getting a good, strong drive step because that good, strong drive step will lead naturally into a good, airborne step/hop into the ball.

Placekickers come to understand that, since height and accuracy are more important than distance on extra points and short field goals (up to 35 yards), they should err on the side of being too close to the ball at impact rather than too far from it. Therefore, they learn to adjust their steps accordingly. Until a placekicker becomes comfortable with, and adept at, marking off his steps and making the minor adjustments required by distance kicks, it is wise to give the holder the responsibility for gaining distance (see Chapter 6, "The Placekicking Team"). Some new students remark after the first couple of practices that kicking is a lot more complicated than it appears. That is true, if the player is serious about kicking, if he wants to kick the ball well every time, and if he wants to kick the ball farther and more accurately with less effort.

Be careful that you do not inadvertently end up in a situation where both the kicker and holder make an adjustment such that the kicker ends up kicking a low line-drive with little or no accuracy. Minor adjustments to the placekicker's measurements may be needed to ensure that his kicking foot consistently makes proper contact with the ball. For example, if he repeatedly finds that he is not getting enough height on his kicks, he needs to move slightly closer to the ball by marking his steps, then moving his plant foot one to three inches closer to the ball. This adjustment will ensure that his kicking foot strikes the ball at a lower point, thereby getting more lift. If the placekicker is getting too much height (the ball spins too quickly end-over-end), or if he wants to add distance to his kicks, he needs to move his plant foot an additional one to three inches away from the ball so he will strike the ball at a higher point. Note that it is the starting point, the distance from where the ball will be spotted, that determines height and distance, not a change in kicking mechanics.

Coaching Tip: The placekicker must mark off a slightly longer approach when kicking off a placekicking block or a kickoff tee than he will when kicking off the ground, in order to compensate for the difference in the ball's position. For example, steps marked off for a teed-up ball (usually one to two inches off the ground) will result in the placekicker being too far away from a ball spotted on the ground because of the difference in height. Thus, whereas he will kick a teed-up ball well, he will top the ball and line drive it when it is placed directly on the ground.

Foot Contact

The basics of foot contact are as follows:
- Distance is gained by striking the ball slightly above the sweet spot (a third of the way from the bottom of the ball).
- Height is gained by striking the ball slightly below the sweet spot.
- Accuracy is gained by striking the ball more fully, and is more often achieved with height than with distance.

Sometimes, when a placekicker is having trouble getting comfortable with the one-and-a-half-step approach, the culprit is informational overload. He is focusing on the initial step, the plant, and the foot contact, thereby making the kicking process more difficult. It is simply a case of the placekicker trying to do everything right, but getting nothing, or not enough, right. This situation is fairly natural, one that occurs in every sport as an athlete tries to unlearn bad habits and learn basic fundamentals. Until kicking properly becomes second nature, his frustration may mount to the point where he either reverts to his original error-prone and inconsistent approach, bears down even more, or gives up completely.

When the player is frustrated, have him kick the ball with only a half-step approach. The placekicker should imagine that he is trying quickly to kick a soccer ball to another player suddenly breaking downfield about 30 yards away. He would not take a full one-and-a-half-step approach, wind up, and kick the ball. Rather, he would simply stroke the ball down the field with a half-step approach because he would not have time to do anything more. Yet he would still be able to consistently place the ball in front of his teammate with little effort or forethought. To use the half-step approach when kicking a football, the kicker should mark off his steps with two rather than three steps (his kicking foot will end up closer to the ball), and then move up about two to four inches. The back leg (the leg that will ultimately become the plant leg) should be a full stride from the kicking leg. The kicker should rock back and forth slightly to help generate the necessary momentum into the kick. The resulting approach will be more balanced, since less forward momentum will be generated. The football will fly at 75 to 80 percent of the height and distance the kicker would normally get with a full one-and-a-half-step approach. If it is more, it is a sign that the placekicker has been getting virtually nothing out of his first step. Remember, the idea is to reinforce the fact that the combination of proper form and the placekicker's natural leg strength will generate more than enough power and accuracy.

Coaching Tip: Aside from helping your kickers overcome informational overload, the two-step kick provides another, very important benefit: namely, instilling your kickers with the confidence to kick even when, due to a bad snap and/or a bad hold, the ball is not ready when they begin their approach. For example, a sophomore high school kicker with limited placekicking experience in game conditions was called upon to kick a 37-yard field goal. Reacting to a poor snap, the kicker stopped his approach after only one step, and then restarted his approach when the ball was finally placed on the tee. The kick sailed cleanly over the crossbar so well that it would have been good from at least 45 yards. One of the reasons he was able to kick the ball so well was because the numerous two-step kicks he had made in practice from that distance gave him the confidence to continue with this attempt rather than abandoning it and hoping something could be made out of the broken play.

One of the most effective ways to teach proper follow-through is to dangle a soft, lightweight object from the crossbar. The object (e.g., an empty, plastic gallon milk container or a plastic bag filled with old rags) should hang between four and five feet above the ground so that only a placekicker using the proper follow-through can kick the object when standing a few feet in front of it (see Figures 1-1 through 1-7).

Figure 1-1

Figure 1-2

Figure 1-3

12

Figure 1-4

Figure 1-5

Figure 1-6

Figure 1-7

When the placekicker is able to kick the target consistently, place a football on a tee behind the object. By using the proper follow-through, he should be able to kick the ball while still kicking the object. The ball's resistance will, of course, make this task more difficult, but not necessarily impossible. (Note: The placekicker should concentrate on his follow-through, not on kicking the ball.) It is likely that he will not strike the ball perfectly, but that is acceptable during this stage. As he improves both his steps and his follow-through, he will begin striking the ball more completely and, after diligent practice, will hit the target and kick the ball well.

Most kicking practices should start with this exercise, especially with those kickers who have the most trouble kicking up and through the ball. Get the most out of this exercise by hanging two objects, one at either end of the crossbar. Four kickers can then benefit from the exercise. Kickers 1 and 2 can kick with the hanging objects to Kickers 3 and 4, who retrieve the balls and kick them back to Kickers 1 and 2. When Kickers 1 and 2 are consistently kicking the object and the ball well, they trade places with Kickers 3 and 4.

The next step is to have the placekicker attempt to kick the ball over the crossbar from a distance of only five to seven yards (10 to 12 yards if kicking off the ground since it is harder to get the proper height when kicking directly off the ground). Yes, this task is difficult to accomplish. However, the intent is not so much to kick the ball over the crossbar as it is to ingrain in the placekicker the habit of kicking up and through rather than just punching the ball. If straight-on kickers are following through properly, their kicks will hit or sail just over the crossbar. Soccer-style kicks typically hit or sail just under the crossbar. As the kicker becomes more proficient, make the exercise more difficult by moving him even closer to the crossbar.

Coaching Tip: Be sure that your experienced kickers do not try to take advantage of their knowledge that moving closer to the ball results in a higher kick. Make sure they kick the ball over the crossbar because they are using the proper follow-through, not because they are cheating on their measurements.

Next, have the placekicker kick the ball from the sideline no more than five yards from the end line (see Figures 1-8 and 1-9). After kicking several times from this spot, move either to the opposite side of the field (to simulate kicking from either hash), or simply stay on the same side of the field, but kick from a spot five yards past the end line.

Once the kickers have kicked from the severe angle enough that they have become more proficient at kicking the ball through the uprights, have them kick directly from the end line about 10 to 15 yards from the uprights (see Figures 1-10 through 1-12). The object is to kick the closest upright, something kickers, if they have been working hard at the severe-angle kicks, will find they can do much more consistently than they thought possible.

Figure 1-8

Figure 1-9

16

Figure 1-10

Figure 1-11

Figure 1-12

Coaching Tip: End-line kicking is a way of introducing a little fun into your kicking practices, something that you must find a way to inject in every kicking practice. If not, your kickers will become bored, frustrated, or both, and eventually find excuses for not practicing well or practicing at all. Then, all your coaching and all their practicing will have been wasted.

Severe-angle placekicking is very important because it reinforces two things: first, the importance of form and follow-through, and second, the importance of setting up at the proper angle from the direction of the kick. Added benefits of introducing the severe-angle kick to practice sessions, of course, are that the increased distance goes a long way towards satisfying the placekicker's natural desire or need to show he can kick for distance, and kicking from within the hash marks seems easy.

Coaching Tips: Severe-angle kicking uses so little practice space that kickers can kick more frequently during practices without disrupting the rest of the team's drills. Do not allow a placekicker's frustration in learning proper placekicking technique to lead to his giving up on what you are teaching, especially when parents are involved. Parents naturally want to see their child do well, and they often get frustrated when the first thing they see is their child getting worse rather than better under your tutelage.

Plenty of parents talk glowingly about how far their child can kick a football, only to see them struggle during their first several kicking practices as they assimilate all the information about measurements and mechanics. Do not give up. Stick with it. Anytime an athlete is taught the proper way to do something, be it hitting a baseball or a golf ball, shooting free throws, or kicking field goals, he will find himself struggling more and getting less out of his efforts until he understands the method and becomes more comfortable with it. He must unlearn old muscle memory and replace it with new muscle memory. In time, even a slight improvement in technique by the placekicker will result in a significant improvement in accuracy, height, and distance. Be forewarned: this stage can be troublesome if the placekicker feels he has made such progress that he can kick from a serious distance rather than continuing to work on his form and follow-through.

A performance plateau during which the placekicker will see little additional benefit for additional hard work and practice will follow the second phase. It is at this stage that he should be instructed to put more effort into each kick to gain more distance. Be careful, however, because adding effort, putting more oomph into a kick, will result in a loss of form and a resulting decrease in performance.

Work through performance plateaus until both form and effort operate in concert. Keep in mind the following:
- The better the follow-through, the longer the foot is in contact with the ball, and the more force is transferred from the kicking leg and foot to the ball.
- A short follow-through means that the kicking foot actually began slowing down before making contact with the ball, thereby losing considerable power.
- It is simply not possible to suddenly stop the kicking foot immediately after striking the ball.

During performance plateaus, when a kicker cannot seem to get additional distance, he will be tempted to commit the following errors:
- Muscle the ball too much and pull his head and shoulders up too soon, resulting in a topped ball (striking the ball above the sweet spot), with a consequent loss of height, distance (from too little height), and accuracy (depending on which side the ball was struck).
- Take too small of a first step (thereby ending up too far from the ball at contact), resulting in a topped ball, with a consequent loss of height, distance (from too little height), and accuracy (depending on which side the ball was struck).
- Take too big or aggressive of a first step (thereby ending up too close to the ball at contact), resulting in a ball struck below the sweet spot, with a consequent loss of distance (from too much height).

Timing the Approach

Most inexperienced placekickers wait until the holder has spotted the ball before beginning their approach. Depending on the skill of his blockers, or the lack of aggressive defenders, such a placekicker may succeed in getting off his kicks without their being blocked. Typically, however, the ball should be kicked 1.3 to 1.4 seconds from the time the ball is snapped in high school, faster in college and the pros.

Rather than telling the placekicker to hurry his approach, tell him to start his approach when the ball is snapped. Initially, the kicker will tend to lean too far forward and rush his approach, but with continued practice, he will become more adept at starting his approach sooner. Make it easier on the placekicker by using a snap count instead of letting the snapper snap the ball when he is ready or when the holder signals with his hands for the ball to be snapped. That way he knows exactly when the ball will be snapped and exactly when he needs to begin his approach. The more comfortable this routine becomes, the more he will be able to concentrate on approaching and kicking the ball properly rather than on when to begin his approach. Few defenses will be able to figure out the cadence quickly enough during a game to time their rush.

Coaching Tip: Most athletes want to learn how to placekick soccer-style rather than straight-on. Once you become experienced as a placekicking coach, you will be able to tell fairly soon whether or not a given athlete should kick soccer-style or straight-on. Much to many athletes' disappointment, their more natural style, the style that takes greater advantage of their leg strength, is straight-on. One of the easiest ways of separating the straight-on placekickers from the soccer-style placekickers is their foot contact. Most natural straight-on placekickers strike the ball with the kicking foot, off the toe, rather than on the instep. Try as they might, they find it extremely difficult to strike the ball properly whether or not they are able to approach the ball properly. Do yourself, and them, a favor by teaching them the straight-on placekicking style. It is much easier to teach, and much easier to learn.

2

Straight-on Placekicking

Marking Off the Approach

A straight-on kicker should face the ball with the toe of his kicking foot positioned one to three inches directly behind the spot where the ball will be set. He should then take three steps straight back, starting with his plant foot and ending with his feet about five inches apart and the plant foot three to five inches closer to the ball (see Figures 2-1 through 2-5).

Figure 2-1

Figure 2-2

Figure 2-3

Figure 2-4

Figure 2-5

Coaching Tips: The measurement steps should be slightly longer than the placekicker's normal stride. Too often, novice placekickers take unnaturally large strides or steps that are too small. The former leaves them too far from the ball, the latter too close. Either way, their subconscious minds unsuccessfully attempt to compensate for the problem during the approach.

The angle of the steps taken from the ball should mirror the direction the placekicker wants the ball to go. In other words, except when the ball is being kicked from the center of the field, the placekicker should approach the ball on an angle. The kicker will, therefore, line up closer to the left sideline when attempting a kick from the left hash mark and closer to the right sideline when attempting a kick from the right hash (see Figures 2-6 and 2-7).

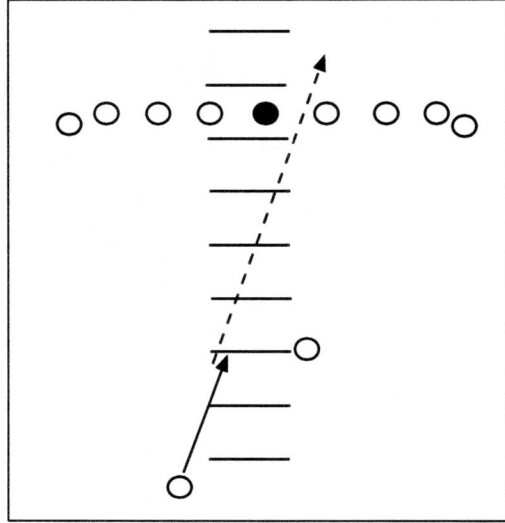

Figure 2-6

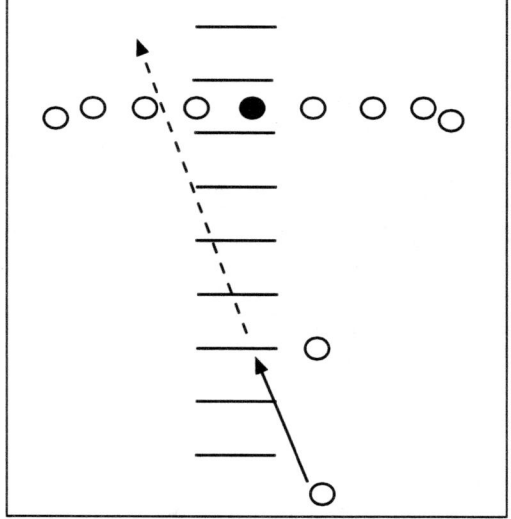

Figure 2-7

Note from Figure 2-5 that the placekicker should lean forward slightly with his upper body. If he leans too much, he may lose his balance in anticipation of the snap, thereby resulting in a small first step. If he leans too little or does not lean at all, his body may jerk forward when he starts his approach.

The Approach

A straight-on kicker must lean forward during his first step, thrusting both arms forward and up (see Figures 2-8 through 2-10). The use of both arms is critical because one arm will not generate the necessary balance and momentum. The placekicker should visualize himself preparing to pull his body forward and through the next step, much as a cross-country skier pulls himself along with each stride.

Figure 2-8

Figure 2-9

Figure 2-10

The second step is, in essence, a half step/half hop, bringing the placekicker to the ball with his kicking leg prepared to make contact (see Figures 2-11 and 2-12). The plant foot will end up to the side of and behind the ball at impact. Note the position of the kicking foot through the approach: it is "locked and loaded" (see Figures 2-12 through 2-15).

Figure 2-11

Figure 2-12

Figure 2-13

Figure 2-14

Figure 2-15

Foot Contact

Straight-on kickers make contact with less surface area of both their kicking foot and the ball than do soccer-style kickers. Thus, a straight-on kicker is at a distinct disadvantage when it comes to generating distance and accuracy, since he has a smaller margin for error (see Figure 2-16), and is more dependent than a soccer-style kicker on his holder to place the ball properly on the desired spot. A straight-on kicker must strike the ball with his toes just below the center of the ball.

Figure 2-16

The Follow-Through

Regardless of whether a player is kicking straight-on or soccer-style, the kicking foot should travel in an arc up and through the ball with the lower half of the leg cocked, then exploding forward through impact. Review Figures 2-13 and 2-14 again. Note that the force of the kicker's follow-through will lift his plant foot completely off the ground (heel first) so that it comes to rest about 6 to 12 inches in front of the spot. His kicking leg should land four to seven inches in front of the plant foot.

Coaching Tips: Use the plant and kicking feet as guides for adjusting your placekicker's form. For example, if the plant foot remains planted after impact, then too little power and follow-through is being generated, probably because the kicker is overly concerned with lifting the ball and/or watching the flight of the ball. If the kicking leg lands too far in front of the plant foot, then the kicker is leaning forward and off-balance due to excessive effort prior to, and during, the kick.

A placekicker is constantly being coached to keep his head down and follow through. How can he do both simultaneously? He cannot since it is impossible to do both. If he keeps his head down, he will "block" or restrict his follow-through and thus his power and accuracy. What he must do is keep his head centered on the ball during the approach, then allow his shoulders to open and his head to come up as his kicking leg comes up and through the ball. Go back to Figures 2-10 through 2-12 and note how the hips and shoulders open up and the head comes up to follow the ball in flight. Note that opening the placekicker's hips and shoulders, and bringing his head up before impact, will result in a poor kick because the kicking foot will naturally be brought through the ball at a higher point.

3

Soccer-Style Placekicking

Marking Off the Approach

The two basic methods for marking a soccer-style kicker's steps start with the kicking foot one to three inches from the ball. As you consider each method, keep in mind the following coaching tips:

   • The steps used to mark off the approach should be slightly longer than the placekicker's normal stride. Too often, placekicking students take unnaturally large strides. The former leaves them too far from the ball, the latter too close. Either way, their subconscious minds unsuccessfully attempt to compensate for the problem during the approach.

   • The angle of the steps taken from the ball should always be 65 to 70 degrees from the direction the kick will go *regardless of where the ball is spotted*. When the ball is being kicked from a hash mark, the placekicker must still approach the ball from a 65- to 70-degree angle. As a result, he'll line up closer to the left sideline when attempting a kick from the left hash mark and closer to the right sideline when attempting a kick from the right hash (see Figures 3-1 and 3-2). This point is *crucial*. Failure to properly measure this angle is why so many soccer-style kickers miss angled field goal attempts. Watch a placekicker on television attempting an angled kick. Most of the time you will be able to tell before he kicks the ball where the ball will go by the angle of his set-up.

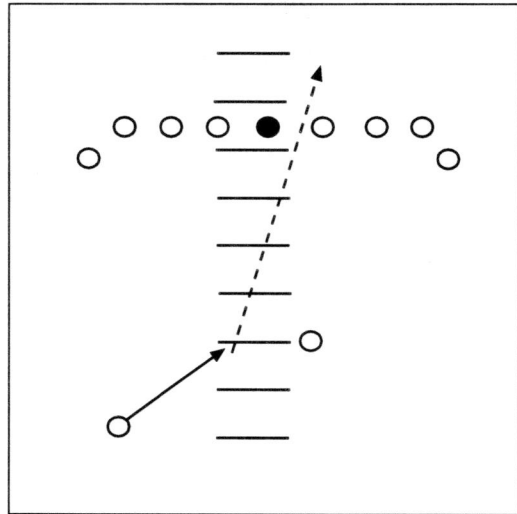

Figure 3-1

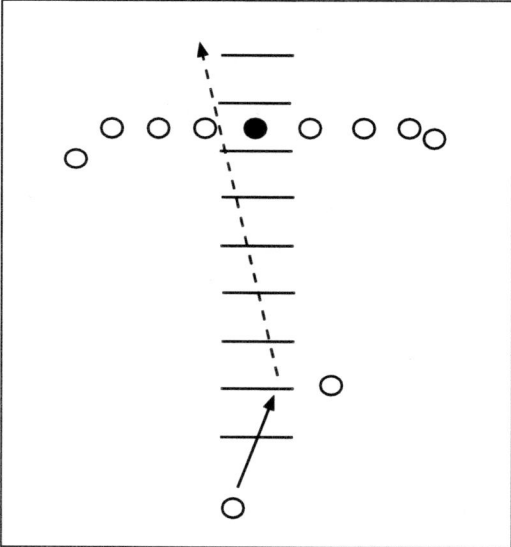

Figure 3-2

Method 1 is the simpler of the two methods and achieves more consistent results. The placekicker takes three steps backwards at a 65- to 70-degree angle (using the same method shown in Figures 2-1 through 2-5). Note that the kicker begins his steps with the toe of his kicking foot positioned one to three inches from the ball. He then steps back first with his plant foot and ends with his kicking foot behind him. Method 2 entails taking three steps straight back (as if the kick were being made by a straight-on kicker), taking two steps to the left or right, depending on whether the placekicker is right- or left-footed, then moving toward the ball six inches (see Figures 3-3 through 3-13).

Figure 3-3

Figure 3-4

Figure 3-5

Figure 3-6

Figure 3-7

Figure 3-8

Figure 3-9

Figure 3-10

Figure 3-11

Figure 3-12

Figure 3-13

It is a matter of simple geometry that Method 2 leaves a kicker farther from the ball than Method 1. Thus, the kicker using Method 2 will have to step up six inches closer to the ball to ensure that he ends up the same distance from the ball. Method 1 is preferable, since due to its fewer "parts," the placekicker is less likely to introduce errors in his measurements. Thus, Method 1 is more likely to consistently result in the desired contact with the ball. However, it must be said that it is more difficult to establish the proper angle from the ball when using Method 1, though proficiency can be gained through practice, repetition, and placekicking exercises that will be discussed later.

A variation of Method 2 is for the two side-steps to be taken at a 70- to 75-degree angle rather an a 90-degree angle, thereby bringing the kicker closer to the ball without having to move six inches closer to the ball after the normal 90-degree side-steps are taken. Obviously, the danger with this Method 2 variation is that now the kicker must make sure that *this* angle is correct otherwise he will be either too close or too far from the ball at set-up. Many kickers use this variation, then suffer through inconsistent kicking, sometimes kicking the ball well, sometimes kicking it short, and sometimes kicking it flat. Remember: simplicity is the key to generating placekicking consistency. Choose a method of measuring your placekickers' steps that produces the same kind of kick every time one is attempted.

Some placekickers prefer to face away from the ball when marking off their steps. However, this variation, facing away from the ball, and then turning around when the steps are completed, only adds more margin for error (some kickers adjust for this problem by stepping back first with their kicking foot when measuring their steps.)

The bottom line, however, is that every placekicker must decide for himself which method he feels most comfortable with, determine which method produces the most consistently positive results, make the necessary adjustments, and practice the method diligently.

Any method of marking off the steps will yield inconsistent results in the beginning when the placekicker is still learning and trying to build muscle memory. Be prepared and willing, however, to adopt a different method if the results from one method do not produce consistently positive results after an adequate amount of practice. For example, many soccer-style placekickers quickly become proficient at Method 1. Others, however, cannot consistently set up at the proper angle. Therefore, their kicks are inconsistent; sometimes they kick well, sometimes they do not. While they kick the ball straight at all times, their poor set-up angle causes the ball to be kicked to one side or the other. Have them adopt Method 2, and their problems are solved. Others have problems adopting Method 2, so switch them to Method 1.

Regardless of the method a soccer-style placekicker uses to mark off his steps, minor adjustments may be needed to ensure that his kicking foot consistently makes proper contact with the ball. For example, if he finds that he is not getting enough height on his kicks, he needs to move slightly closer to the ball by marking his steps, then moving his plant foot one to three inches closer to the ball. This will ensure that his kicking foot strikes the ball at a lower point, thereby getting more lift. If the placekicker is getting too much height on the ball (i.e., the ball spins too quickly end-over-end), or he wants to add distance to his kicks, he needs to move his plant foot an additional one to three inches away from the ball so he will strike the ball at a higher point. Personally, I have had more consistent success marking off my steps properly when kicking off the ground by placing my kicking foot closer to the ball before rather than after marking off my steps. Note that it is the starting point, the distance from where the ball will be spotted, that determines height and distance—not a change in kicking mechanics or more effort on the placekicker's part. Additionally, the longer the field goal that is being attempted, the more important is to adjust the steps accordingly since the margin for error is less.

Coaching Tips: The placekicker must mark off a slightly longer approach when kicking off a placekicking block or a kickoff tee than he will when kicking off the ground in order to compensate for the difference in the ball's position. For example, steps marked off for a teed-up ball — usually one to two inches off the ground — will result in the placekicker being too far away from a ball spotted on the ground because of the difference in height.

The importance of setting up at a proper angle to the ball will increase dramatically the longer the kick that is being attempted for two reasons. One is that increased distance means decreased margin for error. The other reason is that placekickers will naturally put more effort, more oomph into the ball, the longer the kick. That extra effort makes it more likely that they will pull the ball just enough to miss to the left if they are right-footed kickers, or to the right if they are left-footed kickers. An experienced kicker will, therefore, add a bit more angle to his approach when attempting his longest kicks.

The Approach

A soccer-style kicker's inside arm (the right arm for a right-legged kicker) should naturally thrust forward and down, then swing to the side to balance his initial step, while his outside arm should start mid-way down, then swing sharply upward to balance the necessary backward lean (see Figures 3-14 through 3-17). As with a straight-on kicker's approach, the soccer-style placekicker's second step is, in essence, a half step/half hop, bringing the placekicker to the ball with his kicking leg prepared to make contact with the ball (see Figures 3-16 and 3-17). His inside arm should naturally come back, and his outside arm should thrust up and to the outside to counter-balance his second step.

Some placekickers feel more comfortable taking a short step or a stutter step before taking a strong, aggressive drive step. While the added step may provide more balance, momentum, and power, it also takes more time, thus the approach must start sooner or be executed more quickly. The added step also has the potential for adding error; for example, will the stutter step consistently be the same length? A stutter step must be compensated for when marking off the steps by moving three to six inches farther away from the ball. A note of caution: do all you can to keep your kickers from taking the extra step.

Figure 3-14

Figure 3-15

Figure 3-16

Figure 3-17

Foot Contact

A typical novice soccer-style kicker often turns his foot sideways in an attempt to strike the ball with his instep. This common mistake results in a loss of power and accuracy, as well as a greater tendency to top the ball, or strike the ball too far above the sweet spot. A soccer-style kicker's objective is to strike the ball above the instep, actually along the instep bone (first metatarsal) and the edge of the shoelaces. The reason is simple: striking the ball with the instep results in less power, since the foot gives and bends back as it meets the ball, thereby losing power. The foot will not bend back when the toe is pointed, since the foot is "locked."

Coaching Tips: If your placekicker has trouble turning his foot over so that he strikes the ball with his laces rather than his instep, check his angle of approach to the ball. It is not possible to instep the ball when approaching the ball from the proper angle without losing considerable power, height, and accuracy. Increase his angle, even more than the norm if need be, so that he is forced to turn his foot over and kick the ball with the edge of the laces.

You can tell a lot about a kicker's approach from the sound of the ball being struck. A solid kick generated by contact with the metatarsus will have a deeper sound than will a ball stuck (actually slapped) by the instep. As you become experienced coaching kickers, you will only need to concentrate on the approach and the sound of the ball to know where the ball will end up. In fact, your kickers will be able to tell themselves whether or not the kick is good from the feel they get during the approach and after making contact with the ball.

Practice Exercises

The following three exercises help novice soccer-style kickers gain the muscle memory they need to approach and kick the ball properly. None of them involves kicking a football.

Exercise #1

Have the placekicker kick a soccer ball off the ground to a point 30 yards downfield while standing over the ball (i.e., with no run-up at all). He should quickly learn to snap his kicking leg down and through the ball without using his toe, as if he were using a straight-on approach. This tendency is one of the most difficult for placekicking students to unlearn.

Exercise #2

Have the placekicker quickly and repeatedly kick a soccer ball against a wall from no more than 15 yards away. The key to this exercise is that the placekicker not only gets the repetition he needs, the speed and quickness of the exercise forces him to rely on his athleticism, agility, and instincts rather than forethought to strike the ball properly by taking away enough time that he is forced to act and react to the ball.

Coaching Tip: Make sure he does not kick the ball so hard that it caroms off the wall and past him. The idea is to kick it hard enough to be able to kick it again and again and again just as a tennis player hits a tennis ball against a wall.

Exercise #3

Stand with your back to a backstop while rolling a soccer ball to the placekicker, just as if the two of you were playing kick ball. The ball should be rolled so the placekicker is forced to kick it soccer-style. As with the first exercise, the placekicker will more naturally become comfortable kicking with the edge of the laces rather than with his instep.

The Follow-Through

Regardless of whether one is kicking straight-on or soccer-style, the kicking foot should travel in an arc up and through the ball, with the lower half of the leg cocked, then exploding forward through impact (see Figures 3-18 and 3-19). Little power and control are gained by a soccer-style kicker who swipes his kicking leg around and through the ball in a roundhouse motion.

Figure 3-18

Figure 3-19

Note in Figures 3-17 and 3-18 that the placekicker's weight is back rather than forward. If his weight is forward, it is the result of a too-fast and slightly out-of-control approach that will lead to a "blocked" motion, thus limiting distance and accuracy. The soccer-style kicker's plant foot should end up slightly in front of and to the side of the ball rather than behind and to the side of the ball, as a straight-on kicker's plant foot would land. The position of the kicking foot extends out farther as the placekicker nears the ball; it does not remain fixed and unchanged throughout the approach.

Also note that the force of a soccer-style kicker's follow-through will cause his plant foot to roll to the outside, and then turn the toe on the plant foot to the outside. His kicking leg should hang high in midair, outside of the plant foot. If it is done properly, the kicker will be able to stand motionless on only his plant foot while watching the flight of the ball—a result of his follow-through counter-balancing his forward motion.

Coaching Tips: Use the plant and kicking feet as guides for adjusting your placekicker's form. For example:

- If the kicking leg lands in front of the kicker with little leg lift, the kicker was off balance, having either expended too much effort prior to and during the kick (typically on long field-goal attempts), or kept his head down excessively, thereby not allowing his hips and shoulders to open up and rotate.

- If the kicking leg lands to the inside (open stance), the initial step was too strong, thereby generating so much momentum that the kicker was taken past the ball.
- If the kicking leg lands to the outside, the kicker tried to kick the ball too hard, using a roundhouse motion with his kicking leg. As a result, his initial step was too small and/or his plant foot pointed to the outside, sometimes even behind the ball spot.

Now that the placekicker has learned to properly mark off his approach steps and has perfected his form and follow-through, he needs to learn when and how to make adjustments to ensure that he strikes the ball properly in all situations.

4

Adjustments

Kicking from the Hash Marks

Frequently, a field goal is attempted from the hash marks rather than from the center of the field. This technique not only *slightly* lengthens the kick, but the greater angle of the attempt also provides the defense with a greater opportunity to block the kick, or at least tip the ball as it rises. The ball should be spotted closer to the sideline to maximize the distance that the blocking defender coming from the middle of the field must cross to get to the kick (see Figures 4-1 and 4-2).

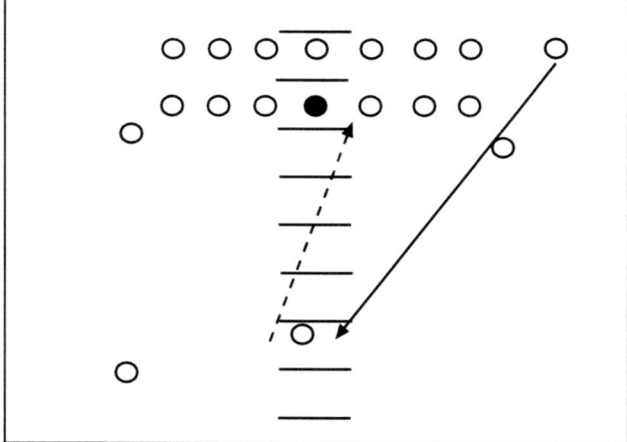

Figure 4-1

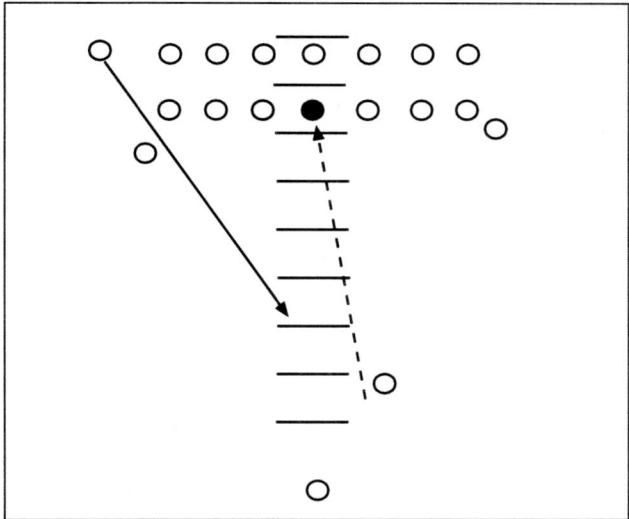

Figure 4-2

Be careful not to move the ball more than one foot outside the hash marks. Anything more will make the snap and the hold too difficult to execute properly. Note that placing the ball directly behind the snapper as would be done when kicking from the middle of the field would give the outside rusher a better chance to reach the kick since the distance he would travel would be reduced at the same time the kick would be traveling towards him. Moving the ball in this manner does shorten the distance the nearside blocking defender must cover to reach the ball, but the ball's flight away from him more than compensates for this "advantage."

Coaching Tips: To avoid, or at least minimize, the problems associated with kicking from the hash marks (especially shorter kicks where the angle of the kick is magnified), be judicious when making your third-down call. For example, running a third-down play into the sideline from the hash mark may not be the best long-term option, since failure to achieve a first down will leave your placekicker with a more difficult field-goal attempt than would have been the case had the play been run to the middle of the field. A word of caution: a coach should consider more factors than simply the difficulty of the field-goal attempt when making a third-down call within field-goal range. Nevertheless, this factor should not be excluded from the decision-making process, especially when working with an inexperienced placekicker, and at the end of either half, when a field goal takes on greater importance.

Consider taking a delay-of-game penalty, an offside penalty, or any other five-yard penalty before attempting a very short kick from the hash marks in order to move the ball back five yards, thereby reducing the angle and difficulty of the kick. You can use this tip in reverse when coaching the team attempting to block the kick. Consider *not* accepting a penalty that would move the kicker back five yards; make him take the most severe angle kick whenever possible.

Slope of the Field

Most football fields are constructed and maintained with a crown down the middle of the field running from end zone to end zone to promote water drainage. Most quarterbacks know how a crown can make sideline routes and out patterns more difficult to complete; the throws tend to fly over the receivers' heads, since the quarterback is throwing from a higher elevation than the receiver. The experienced quarterback compensates accordingly.

A crown affects the field-goal kicker in that he must travel uphill to get to the ball. Traveling uphill means that each approach step will be shorter, which means that the placekicker will end up farther from the ball at impact. The result will be a ball struck closer to the toe, leading to a loss of power and control, and possibly farther up on the ball, leading to a loss of height and control.

The experienced placekicker will compensate for this problem by moving no more than one to two inches closer to the ball when marking off his steps. A portion of pre-game warm-ups should be devoted to making the necessary adjustments and getting comfortable with the different "feel" of an uphill approach.

Mud and Loose Turf

A placekicker should be prepared to make slight adjustments due to the size of the football being kicked. At one time, a major college conference allowed placekickers to bring a practice ball — as long as it was regulation size — into a game to kick. Given that practice balls tend to be slightly larger and more elastic than game balls, practice balls can be kicked farther. Thus, the game ball you are using is probably smaller and stiffer than the practice balls that your kicker has been practicing with all week. Compared the game ball to a regular practice ball and you will be amazed by the size difference. To compensate, have your placekicker moved an inch closer to the ball when measuring kickoffs during games and he should be able to kick the ball farther.

The first thing the placekicker must come to grips with, and accept, when kicking in mud, or on a sodden, slippery field, is that he very well may slip and fall during his attempt. Little can or should be done to prevent what may, admittedly, be an embarrassing and frustrating situation. The placekicker's job is to make the field goal, not avoid embarrassment. The more he thinks about slipping and falling, the more likely he will kick poorly. Short of wearing long-cleated shoes to improve traction, the kicker should find the best spot for his plant foot, carefully mark off his steps, and move slightly closer to the ball to compensate for possible slippage during the approach, and attack the ball as if he were kicking in ideal conditions. Placekickers appreciate this truism about kicking in sloppy conditions: no one will know or understand that a field goal was missed because the placekicker was trying to avoid falling. They will, however, excuse a missed field goal when they see the placekicker slip and fall, and they will greatly applaud the skill and determination of a placekicker who makes a field goal even while slipping and falling. Therefore, placekickers should forget about slipping and falling and just concentrate on kicking naturally.

Serious placekickers use rainy-day practice time to become more comfortable with kicking in poor conditions. They also use pre-game warm-up time to make adjustments necessary for that particular field. Do not pass up the chance to practice kicking in poor conditions, and do not limit that foul weather practice time to just your placekicker. Get your snapper and holder out in the mud or wet grass and get them comfortable with handling their jobs in poor conditions since they will likely have to perform in those conditions at least once during a typical football season.

Artificial Turf

Most placekickers prefer to kick off on artificial turf since they get much better traction. In addition, because the artificial-turf surface is smoother than a grass field, the ball is spotted more cleanly and sits up higher. However, an experienced placekicker will make the necessary adjustments to the downsides of kicking off artificial turf.

First of all, the better traction means that the placekicker will generate more power and momentum during his approach on artificial turf than he will on grass. While that means that less effort will be required to kick the ball the same distance, it also means that the placekicker will end up closer to the ball at impact. The result will be greater height and, consequently, a loss of distance.

The smooth, consistent artificial-turf surface also means that the ball will sit up higher than it will on a grass field, where the tee (or ball, if kicking directly off the ground) sinks down in the grass or sits in a depression between clumps of grass. Therefore, an experienced placekicker will add about an inch to his steps when setting up for the kick.

Coaching Tips: An adjustment made to accommodate the better traction of artificial turf may also provide enough compensation for the increased height of the ball when spotted. A high school or lower-level placekicker's use of a kicking block magnifies the height differential on field-goal and extra-point attempts. Since most of the placekicks attempted at these levels tend to be fairly short, where height rather than distance is the objective, it may not be wise or necessary to make adjustments for artificial turf at these levels.

By now, you should understand how proper placekicking form will compensate for a lack of leg strength. Proper form will enable a recreation-league athlete to placekick consistently from 30 to 35 yards, a high school athlete from 35 to 40 yards, and a college athlete from 40 to 45 yards. In fact, proper form will add 10 yards or more to a player's kicks over what leg strength alone will supply. For example, I have consistently kicked 50-yard field goals off a placekicking block (and 45-yard field goals off the ground) as an out-of-shape 41-year-old (with a knee that has visited four operating rooms), while a strong 18-year-old with a far stronger leg struggles to kick consistently from 45 yards. The obvious reason is that my form, through many years of practice and experience, is more consistent, and makes up for my declining leg strength and flexibility.

Having shown proper form and how to use it consistently, the focus of the following chapter will explain how to improve a placekicker's form by improving his flexibility, and how to effectively improve his leg strength to add distance.

5

Leg Flexibility and Strength

Stretching

Obviously, the greater a placekicker's flexibility, the better his follow-through will be. To the extent that he's flexible, he will be able to stride more crisply towards the ball, reach back farther with his kicking leg on his second step, and kick harder and more fluidly through the ball. The following are basic exercises to use when working with placekickers.

Stretching Notes

- Jog 100 to 200 yards before stretching to warm up the muscles and allow for more complete stretching.
- Never bob or bounce during the stretch, since it will result in inadequately stretched muscles and even muscle pulls. Instead, maintain steady tension on the muscles being stretched.
- Perform three five-second repetitions per exercise, with more reps done if necessary after completing the complete stretching exercise routine.
- Keep the knee straight on the leg being stretched, even if it means the stretch is limited.
- Keep the head down to maximize the stretching of the neck and back muscles. Remember, it is not only the leg muscles that need to be stretched. The back

muscles need to be stretched as well. Try kicking with a sore neck or back and you will quickly understand how important those muscles are to a placekicker. In addition, keeping the head down will automatically allow for greater stretching of the leg muscles.
- Stretch frequently during practices and games; muscles can and will tighten, even during these short periods.
- Do not cheat. Without discomfort, the muscles are not being stretched properly.
- Do not overstretch. Stretching muscles too far will cause intense pain or a burning sensation (they are on the verge of tearing). Common sense is the order of the day, with a focus on gradual improvement rather than quick results.

Modified Hurdler Stretch

The primary objective of the modified hurdler stretch is to stretch the Achilles tendons as well as the hamstring and calf muscles. Most athletes, especially track athletes, use this basic stretching exercise. The placekicker sits on the ground with one leg pointed ahead, heel out and toe up, and the other leg pulled back with the foot pressed against the inside of the opposite knee (see Figure 5-1). Many athletes fail to pull the bent knee back, thereby limiting the value of this exercise. It should be pulled back at a 90-degree angle from the leg being stretched. The foot on the outstretched leg should point skyward to maximize the impact on the Achilles tendon and calf muscles. The placekicker reaches for his upraised toe with both hands, working to touch his nose to his knee. Once this can be accomplished, the placekicker should attempt to touch his nose to the ground on either side.

Figure 5-1

Lay-Back

The primary objective of the lay-back is to stretch the quadriceps, as well as the hip, groin, and stomach muscles. The placekicker sits in the modified hurdler stretch position, then lies back as far as he can, resting his weight on his elbows and/or hands to the extent necessary (see Figures 5-2 and 5-3). As he becomes more flexible, he will be able to lie back farther. Move directly from the modified hurdler stretch to the lay-back. For convenience, simply alternate back and forth between the two.

Figure 5-2

Figure 5-3

Tuck

The primary objective of the tuck is to stretch the hip, groin, neck, and back muscles. The placekicker sits on the ground, grabs his feet, and pulls them towards him (see Figures 5-4 and 5-5). Note that the feet and head are tucked in tightly to maximize the stretching benefit. Use an assistant to push down on the kicker's shoulders to increase the stretch if need be.

Figure 5-4

Figure 5-5

"V"

The primary objective of the "V" is to stretch the Achilles tendons, as well as the hamstring and groin muscles. The placekicker is seated on the ground with his legs splayed out in the form of a "V" (see Figure 5-6). The feet should point skyward to maximize the impact on the Achilles tendons and calf muscles. This exercise can be done while standing, but it is preferably done on the ground to maximize the impact on the back muscles and minimize the strain on the leg muscles. The placekicker stretches toward his right foot with both hands, then repeats the stretch to the left (see Figures 5-7 and 5-8). Then, he leans forward between his legs, reaching each hand toward the same-side foot (see Figure 5-9).

Figure 5-6

Figure 5-7

Figure 5-8

Figure 5-9

Coaching Tip: Add another stretch to your placekicker's routine by bringing his feet together after finishing the "V" stretch, then touching his toes; remember to keep the head down to stretch the neck and back muscles. Then place one leg over the other, stretch, switch the legs, and stretch. These additional stretches serve as safer alternatives than the standing versions so often used by athletes because most of the weight of the upper body, and the strain it places on the leg muscles, has been taken away.

Side-to-Side

The primary objective of the side-to-side is to stretch the hip, upper hamstring, and groin muscles. The placekicker is standing and spreads his legs to either side, with both feet pointing to the side (see Figure 5-10). He then shifts his weight to one side, placing one hand on his stretched knee until he feels his hamstring and groin muscles stretching on his extended leg (see Figures 5-11 and 5-12). The player should not place most of the upper body's weight on the bent knee via the other hand or elbow. This position will transfer too much weight to the side, thereby taking the pressure off the targeted muscles. As simple as this exercise is, it is often the most difficult of the stretching exercises for the uninitiated to grasp. Often, the athlete turns his feet in the direction of the stretch, rather than to the side, and rests his weight on the bent knee.

Figure 5-10

Figure 5-11

Figure 5-12

Strength Training

Again, the reason a placekicker should strengthen his legs is to gain more power and drive through the ball with the same amount of effort. In other words, a placekicker who uses the same form and improves his leg strength will naturally add distance and height to his kicks, but a placekicker who sacrifices good form by trying to kick the ball harder is susceptible to losses in both distance and accuracy.

Weight training, of course, has a place in a placekicker's practice regimen, but it need not be a particularly intense or significant one. It is far more important for a placekicker to strengthen his muscles through actual kicking, and other forms of muscle-straining exercise. After all, the soreness that is felt in the groin, calf, and upper hamstring muscles after the early placekicking practice sessions is a direct result of exercising muscles that have not previously been used. Muscles strengthened through non-weight training methods remain longer and more flexible, thereby retaining the smooth freedom of movement that proper form requires. However, this book shall outline a simple weight-training program.

A placekicking training regimen combines kicking, running, and bleacher work. Running two to three miles, particularly along hilly terrain, will strengthen and tone the leg muscles without producing the muscle bulk that restricts movement. A placekicker should do roadwork every other day or every third day to avoid getting shin splints and ruining his form by tiring his legs.

A consistent routine of bleacher work produces strong calf muscles and quadriceps, thereby increasing the power needed for the initial, driving approach step, as well as the kick itself. Bleacher work consists of hopping up the first aisle on two feet and then jogging back down and over to the next aisle. The placekicker hops up the aisle on one foot, then walks back down and over to the next aisle (to minimize stress on the knees) and jogs to the next aisle. As he gets in better shape, the placekicker will be able to follow this routine completely around the stadium, going higher up the aisles each time.

When stadium seating is not available, have your placekickers hop on one leg as high as possible for ten yards, then switch legs and hop back. Since the object is to jump as high as possible, speed is not important. Both legs must be worked since both legs provided the drive necessary to kick well. In addition, have your placekickers stride out at a distance of about two times their normal stride, then slowly lower their back knee almost to the ground, then stride out again. Their hands should remain at their sides so as to maintain the proper balance as well as to ensure that their legs are doing all the work, unassisted by their hands pushing down on their knees (see Figures 5-13 through 5-21).

Figure 5-13

Figure 5-14

Figure 5-15

Figure 5-16

Figure 5-17

Figure 5-18

Figure 5-19

Figure 5-20

Figure 5-21

The first time your kickers start doing these exercises, they will likely snicker that neither is difficult. Once they have done them repeatedly for several minutes, though, they will appreciate how well these simple exercises strengthen their legs. In fact, they quickly become difficult to execute as the muscles become strained. An important side benefit, especially when the athlete's sole responsibility is placekicking, is that when he has worked hard and long enough to do the hopping and lunging in sequence completely around the practice field, he will have gained the respect of his fellow teammates.

Leg strengthening should not be confined to practice time. During games, a placekicker should make a habit of hopping in place on one foot, then both feet, as his team's offense nears field-goal range. This simple exercise helps to warm up the muscles (making stretching easier and more effective), as well as to pump up the muscles (providing the power needed for long kicks). Resistance training is another important component of leg strengthening. Here, the placekicker is pushing or pulling against a stationary object or elastic material. The placekicker has a variety of options.

Ball Squeeze

The placekicker sits in a chair with a ball between his knees. He presses in while counting to five, and then relaxes (see Figure 5-22). He repeats this several times, alternating the size and elasticity of the ball, if possible. This exercise should also be done while lying on one's back to strengthen different muscles (see Figure 5-23). While this exercise is useful to straight-on and soccer-style kickers, it tends to benefit soccer-style kickers more.

Figure 5-22

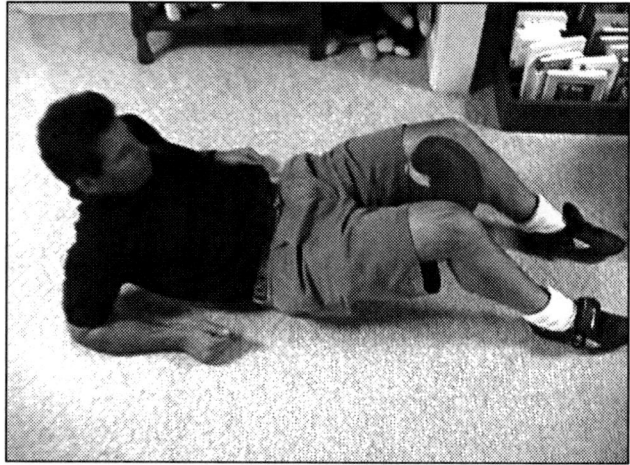
Figure 5-23

Door Jamb or Wall

This exercise is done while standing to maintain the necessary balance. The individual pushes out against a door jamb or wall, holding the position to a count of five, relaxing, then repeating several times (see Figure 5-24). The individual then repositions himself so that he is pushing in on the door jamb (see Figure 5-25).

Figure 5-24

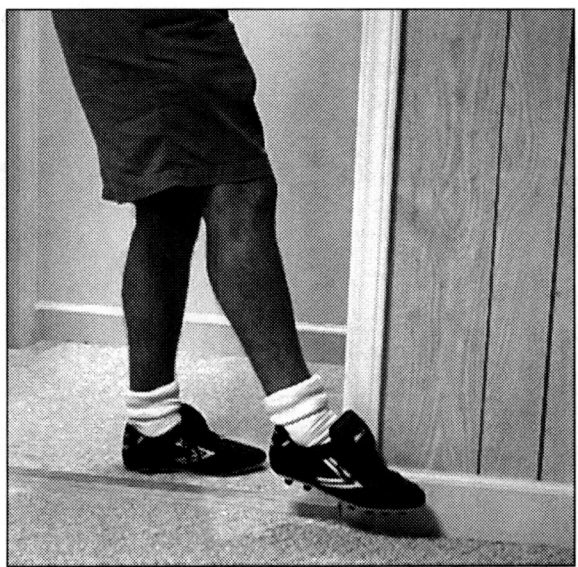

Figure 5-25

Assistance

The following exercises require an assistant.

Lying on the Stomach

The placekicker lies on his stomach and, while keeping his knee on the ground, pulls one foot up past 90 degrees as an assistant generates resistance by pulling down on the foot (see Figure 5-26). The exercise is then reversed, with the placekicker pushing down against resistance generated by the assistant (see Figure 5-27).

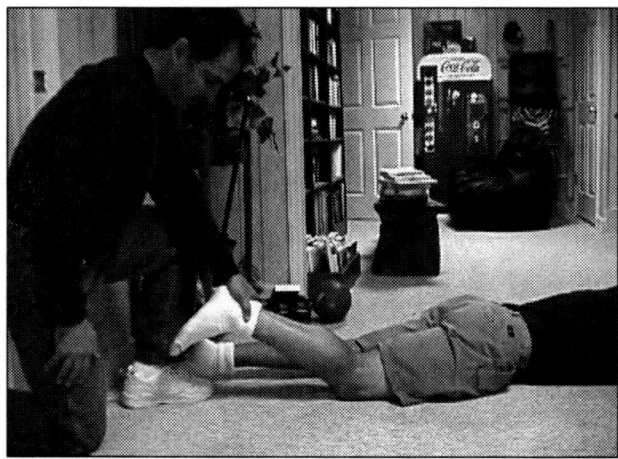

Figure 5-26

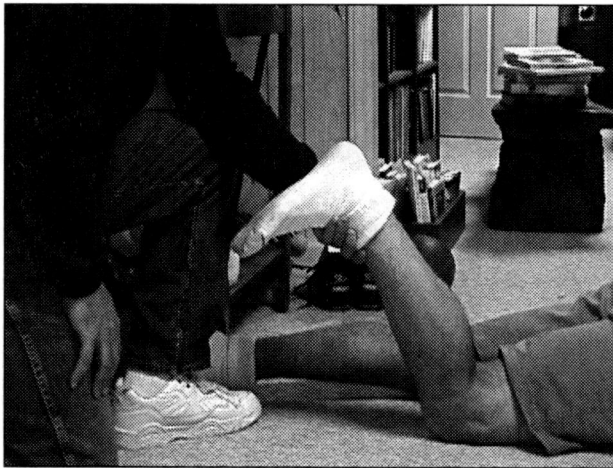

Figure 5-27

Coaching Tip: Resistance should be applied evenly so that the leg is pulled up and down in a smooth arc.

Sitting

Against an assistant's resistance, the placekicker pushes his foot up while keeping his knee down, then pulls his foot back (see Figures 5-28 and 5-29). Both of these exercises can be done against a stationary object or with the aid of an elastic strap. A serious placekicker need not limit his resistance training to these exercises and can devise any number of additional resistance-based exercises.

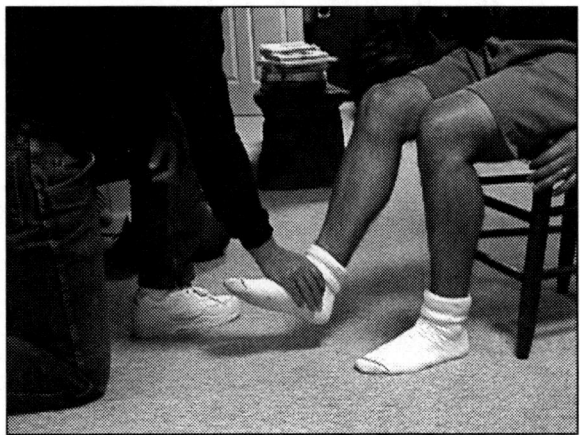

Figure 5-28

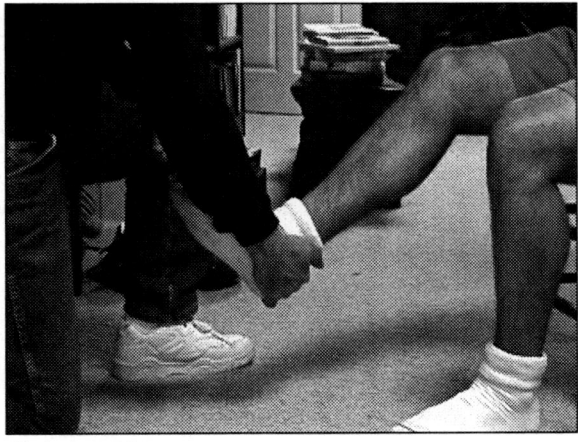

Figure 5-29

Again, weight training should consume the least amount of leg-strengthening activity to avoid developing the tight, bulky muscles that limit flexibility, restrict movement, and inhibit form. In moderation, press lifts can be used, with the seated athlete pushing against a lever that raises a weight. Knee lifts can also be used for the weight-training version of the third set of resistance training exercises. Most weight rooms have the necessary machines.

6

The Placekicking Team

Coaches typically focus on the placekicker only during kicking practices (that is, if they focus on anything related to placekicking). So do the fans during the games, for that matter. After all, when a kick is missed, it is the placekicker's fault, right? Not necessarily. A poor snap or a poor hold will often lead to missed field goals for several reasons, not the least of which is that they divert a placekicker's attention from the task at hand, namely kicking a field goal or an extra point. The problem is that most fans and coaches will not notice that a poor kick was caused by a slightly off-kilter hold; they will automatically, yet understandably, blame the kicker.

Coaching Tip: The importance of a good hold increases as the length of the field goal attempt increases, since the margin for error decreases with distance. To do his job properly and consistently, a placekicker must have complete confidence in his teammates to do their jobs smoothly and flawlessly.

The Snapper

Find a confident, fearless athlete who can toss, not *fire*, a football seven yards in a tight spiral with a flick of his wrist, and you have found a perfect placekicking snapper. Be forewarned, it is not an easy task. Finding a snapper for placekicking is far more difficult than finding a quality punt snapper, given placekicking's dependence on multiple-player precision and timing, as well as the far greater importance of snapping accuracy over speed and distance. In fact, many punt snappers are not able to rein in their snaps well enough and end up firing the ball through their holders' hands.

The snapper should set his feet a little more than shoulder-width apart and far enough behind the ball so that he can comfortably reach it without shifting his weight off his legs and on to the ball. In other words, he should be balanced over the ball and be able to stand up and squat back down without falling either forward or backward. The ball may be gripped with one hand or two, depending on the snapper's skill and comfort level. If one hand is used, the ball should first be positioned properly with both hands so the snapping hand grips the laces under the ball. The off-hand should then be rested on the ground for added balance (see Figure 6-1). The ball is then snapped between the snapper's legs in a soft, straight line to a point no more than 18 inches above the intended spot. If two hands are used to snap the ball, the snapping hand should grip the laces under the ball while the off-hand rests on the other end and on top of the ball (see Figure 6-2).

Figure 6-1

Figure 6-2

The Holder

The holder should be a fluid, confident athlete with good, soft hands and the ability and presence of mind to act quickly in the event of a bad snap or fumbled hold. Typically, skill position players such as quarterbacks, receivers, and defensive backs are used as holders.

The holder can prepare for the snap in either of two ways. The holder and the placekicker should decide on the method that feels most comfortable to both of them, though the placekicker's preference should carry more weight. For example, the holder may set up by kneeling with the leg closest to the placekicker and the other leg stretched out toward the snapper (see Figure 6-3). Experienced holders take this approach further by sitting on their back foot so as to be closer to the intended placement. The holder may also set up by kneeling with the leg farthest from the placekicker (see Figure 6-4). An experienced holder makes this method more comfortable by sitting on his back foot.

Figure 6-3

Figure 6-4

Coaching Tips: The holder should remain relaxed and should not stretch too far forward for the ball (see Figures 6-5 and 6-6). His elbows must not be locked because locked elbows do not provide the necessary give or cushion when catching the ball. The holder should kneel approximately six inches from the intended placement so he'll neither crowd the placekicker nor have to reach so far that he leans heavily on the ball. He should center his knee by the intended spot. If he sets up in front of the spot, he's likely to place the ball too far forward. If he sets up behind the spot, he's likely to place the ball too far back.

Figure 6-5

Figure 6-6

Regardless of where and how the holder positions his legs, he should always spot the ball with the hand closest to the kicker (the left hand for right-footed placekickers, the right hand for left-footed placekickers), as shown in Figures 6-7 and 6-8, in order to keep the placekicker's view of the ball both unrestricted and free of distraction, and to enable the holder to spin the ball more smoothly and with as little effort as possible. Most football fans know that a straight-on (and, to a lesser degree, a soccer-style) placekicker abhors kicking the laces because the uneven surface reduces the likelihood that the ball will be struck cleanly.

Figure 6-7

Figure 6-8

Coaching Tip: Make sure your holder is not spin-happy. More often than not, the ball does not need to be spun. Adjust the snapper's grip if the laces are a consistent problem, rather than requiring your holder to spin the ball. If the snapper is always snapping the ball at the same speed to the same height and distance and the laces always need to be spun away, have the snapper grip the ball without the laces. A much more common problem, however, is a ball placed off-line in any direction from the intended spot. For example:

- If the ball is spotted too close to the placekicker, it will be struck below the sweet spot, resulting in too much height and a consequent loss of distance.
- If the ball is spotted too far from the placekicker, it will be struck above the sweet spot, resulting in too little height and a higher potential for a blocked kick.
- If the ball is spotted too close to the holder, it will be struck off the side of a straight-on kicker's toe and off the end of a soccer-style kicker's foot, resulting in a loss of power and accuracy.
- Finally, if the ball is spotted too far from the holder, it will be struck off the other side of a straight-on kicker's toe and off a soccer-style kicker's ankle, resulting in a loss of power and accuracy.

Only plenty of practice will ensure a proper placement for professional and collegiate placekicking, since the use of a kicking block on which the placekicker and holder can focus is not permitted. However, the use of a kicking block at the high school, junior high, and recreation-league levels makes it easier to spot the ball properly.

Coaching Tip: Make it even easier to spot the ball correctly at the high school and lower levels by placing a small piece of trainer's tape on the kicking block or by making an "X" with two short pieces of tape. Not only does the tape make it easier for the holder to spot the ball properly, it also gives the placekicker something to focus on during his approach before the ball has been spotted.

It is not only *where* the ball is spotted that is important, it is *how* the ball is spotted. For example, tilting the ball:
- Back will add distance. However, if the tilt is excessive or done without the placekicker's knowledge, the result will be a lower-than-normal kick and a loss of distance. If the placekicker adjusts his steps for a longer kick, a tilted ball will magnify his adjustment and cause the ball to be struck too far above the sweet spot.
- Forward will cause a loss of accuracy, height, and distance, since the ball will be struck too far above the sweet spot.
- Toward the holder will decrease a straight-on kicker's accuracy, but increase the amount of the ball's surface struck by a soccer-style kicker, thereby adding both height and distance with no added effort by the placekicker (see Figure 6-9).
- Away from the holder will decrease a straight-on kicker's accuracy, and result in the ball being struck by a soccer-style kicker's ankle, resulting in a loss of control, height, and distance.

To enable your holder to understand exactly how to spot the ball, have the placekicker measure off his steps, and then direct the holder to tilt the ball in the necessary way. Have the holder look at the ball and get accustomed to exactly how the ball should look when held properly. Then have the holder tilt the ball back to where it was before being tilted so he can see the difference. Have him practice spotting the ball without a snap, then tilting the ball while the placekicker watches from his place three steps away.

Figure 6-9

Coaching Tip: If necessary, the holder can place the ball at different spots. For example, spotting the ball farther from the snapper will result in a shorter, higher kick, while spotting the ball closer to the snapper will result in a longer, lower kick.

The Blockers

After the snapper sets his feet, the kicking team should align itself (as shown in Figure 6-10) with the feet of each interior lineman no more than three inches from the feet of the lineman next to him. The first move each lineman should make is an aggressive thrust off his inside leg and behind the adjacent lineman's outside leg (see Figure 6-11). Note that the result is a low, unbroken barrier extending out from the snapper.

Coaching Tip: The linemen's weight should be forward, not to the side or on their heels. If not, they will be unable to withstand the blockers' surge and will topple backward, allowing gaps through which the blockers can charge on their way to the kicker.

The Backs

A blocking back should be positioned off the outside leg of each tight end. Since a back's responsibility is to prevent inside penetration, he will first block to the inside, then, if necessary, to the outside to maximize the distance the outside rusher must travel to reach the kick.

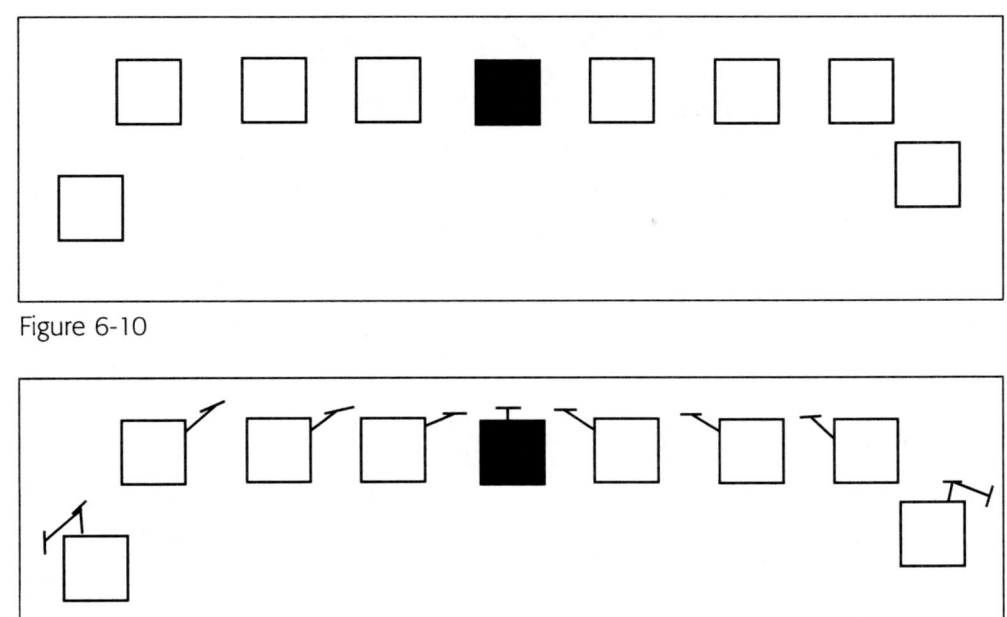

Figure 6-10

Figure 6-11

Coaching Tip: It is not necessary, nor is it advisable, to attempt to fully block the outside rusher. He need only be diverted a step off his intended path to render him ineffective.

Snapping the Ball

A snap count is preferable, since it enables the holder and placekicker to more accurately anticipate when the ball is being snapped and to time his approach. Some coaches let the snapper decide, and some let the holder decide, using a flick of his hands or fingers to signal to the snapper.

Coaching Tips: Whichever method is chosen, the selection should be based on the kicker beginning his approach:
- When the ball is snapped, not after the holder catches the snap or after the ball is spotted.
- In a relaxed fashion with his weight evenly distributed. A kicker who waits impatiently for the ball to be snapped or is surprised when the ball is snapped is ill prepared to do his job properly. He will either stumble because he is leaning too far forward in anticipation of the snap or will jerk backward, then forward before starting his approach. Either way, he will not have the necessary balance or fluidity, nor will he be concentrating on the actual kick.

Fake Field Goals

Every placekicking team should have at least three basic plays executed from the field-goal formation, and these should be practiced during at least one practice session every week. The most commonly used and most effective fake field-goal plays are the holder bootleg, holder sprint-out, and kicker sprint-out.

Coaching Tip: The primary option on all fakes should be the run (especially in short-yardage situations), since the pass option carries with it more opportunities for failure: the pass, the catch, and the run after the catch.

Holder Bootleg

The holder places the ball on the spot, and then quickly picks it up as the kicker begins his fake attempt. The holder then spins and sprints to the outside, where he has the option of running or throwing to one of three possible receivers (see Figure 6-12). The kicker should block any backside rusher after faking the kick.

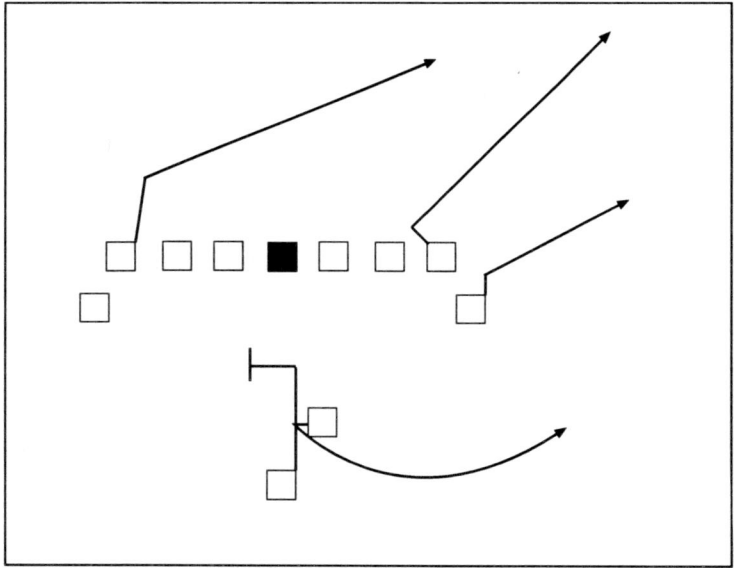

Figure 6-12

Holder Sprint-Out

The holder places the ball on the spot, and then quickly picks it up after the kicker begins his fake attempt. The holder then sprints straight to the outside, where he has the option of running or throwing to one of three possible receivers (see Figure 6-13). The kicker should block any backside rusher after faking the kick. Note: You can modify this play by having your holder simply stand up and throw the ball rather than having him sprint out.

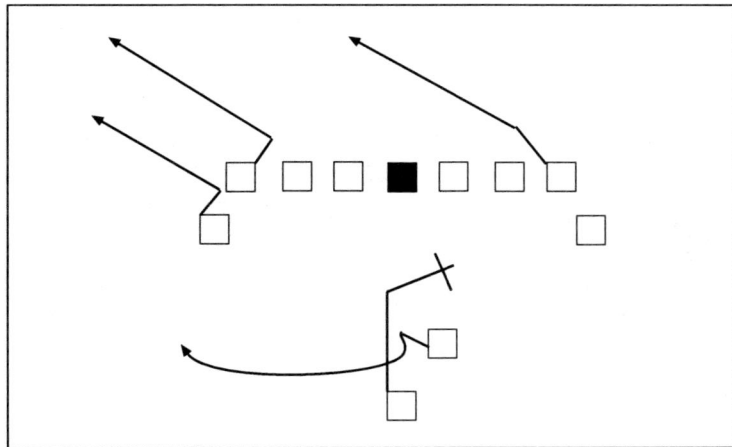

Figure 6-13

Kicker Sprint-Out

Since the goal is to get the kicker to the outside as quickly as possible, the ball is snapped over the holder's head when a straight-on kicker is involved, and over the tee when a soccer-style kicker is involved. The kicker breaks to the outside at the snap, catching the ball and continuing to run, with the option of running or throwing (see Figure 6-14). The holder fakes a catch and a spot, and then blocks the backside rusher. This play requires an athletic placekicker, since the burden for executing the play properly rests squarely on the kicker's shoulders.

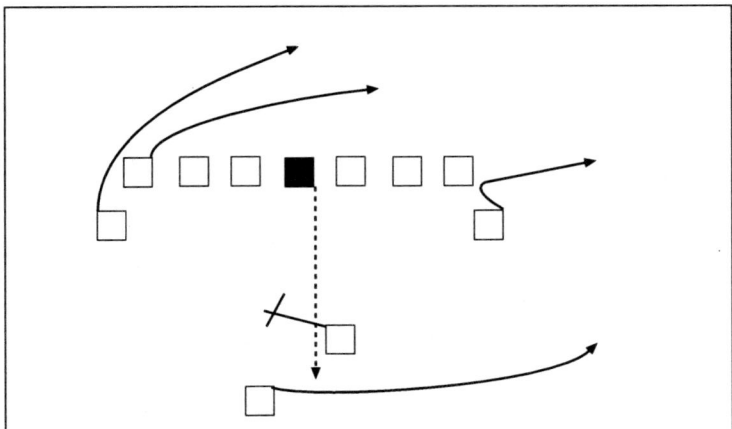

Figure 6-14

Coaching Tips: This play should only be attempted when the placekicker can legitimately throw the ball, the placekicker has the necessary speed to reach the outside, and, most importantly, you are willing to take the risk of your placekicker getting hurt. This last concern, the placekicker getting hurt, brings to mind another major oversight of many football programs. Many coaches struggle to develop two placekickers and so they neglect to develop two holders and two snappers. Do not neglect your snapper and holder back-ups since your first-team snapper and holder are frequently first-team position players and so are prone to injury. Teams get in the position of having to rely on a second-team snapper and holder in the middle of a close contest. They then pay the price for not having given these players sufficient practice time with crucial missed extra points or field goals or even with interceptions that were the result of having to score a touchdown because of the inability to kick even a short field goal.

7

Kickoffs

Often, the kickoff is the most poorly used defensive opportunity. The idea should be to ensure that the opponent's offense starts at the worst field position possible. Most of the time, football fans assume that this means the kicker should kick the ball as hard as he can and try to get the ball into the end zone for a touchback. Maybe so, but would you not prefer to have the offense start on its 15-yard line rather than its 20-yard line as it would in the case of a touchback? And what about daring the kickoff receiving team to handle the ball and return it against a ferocious, head-hunting kickoff team? The point is that a coach should consider all the kickoff options available to him before automatically making a decision to kick the ball deep. Kickoff specialists should understand that not kicking deep does not mean that the kicker cannot kick the ball deep.

Coaching Tips: Kick off from the middle of the field—not the hash marks—in order to:
- Give the kicker more room to work with on deep and deep corner kicks, thereby making it easier to keep the ball inbounds, avoid a penalty for kicking the ball out-of-bounds, and keep the return team guessing as to where the ball will be kicked.
- Allow the ball on pooch, squib, and onside kicks more room to take a bad bounce. For example, an onside kick must travel 10 yards before the kicking team can touch it. Kicking to the short side of the field leaves less room for the ball to go 10 yards before it goes out-of-bounds, far too little room for the kicking team to have a reasonable chance to recover it.

Kicking Deep

Oh, what a beautiful sight a long, end-over-end kickoff can be. And what an easy kick it is to return for major yardage. The long kickoff is both overused and poorly used. First of all, length is not as important as height. Kicking a line drive to a waiting return man can never be as effective for the kicking team as a kickoff 5 to 10 yards shorter that takes longer to come down or even a line drive kickoff that is kicked away from the return men. Work with your kickoff specialists; find out not only how far they can kick the ball, but also how high and how accurately.

Marking off the Steps

A nine-step mark-off on kickoffs provides enough room to build the controlled momentum needed to get a decent kickoff. However, that should be the maximum number of steps your placekicker should take. Mark off the kickoffs the same way you do with field-goal attempts.

Straight-on Kicker

It is impossible for a straight-on kicker to disguise his intent to kick the ball at an angle. However, that does not mean the kickoff receiving team has to know what kind of kickoff is being attempted. Angle the approach away from the direction the kick is intended to travel.

Soccer-Style Kicker

An experienced soccer-style kicker will either decrease or increase the angle of his approach as he kicks the ball to one side of the field or the other. Given that soccer-style kickers line up at an angle to begin with and that few people can kick soccer-style, it is rare that an opposing coach or player will notice an adjustment that a soccer-style kicker makes when kicking toward a sideline—at least not soon enough to react accordingly and in a timely fashion.

Approach

The approach for kickoffs should differ from that used for field goals in only one respect: length. A word of caution: momentum should be built gradually; kickers should not race to the ball.

Proper Form and Follow-Through

Due to the additional momentum generated by the longer run-up, the greater need for power, and the negligible need for accuracy, the kickoff specialist should focus on kicking through the ball rather than concerning himself with a high follow-through. The kicking leg will rarely come more than two feet off the ground, and the plant foot will come off the ground, landing one to two yards downfield rather than staying in place, as it does on placekicks. Most good kickoff specialists will find themselves five yards down field before they are able to stop their forward momentum after kicking off.

Squib Kicks

Executed properly, the squib kick will travel in the air 20 to 30 yards downfield as a low knuckleball. The ball should drop between the lines of the kickoff receiving team, forcing some of the kickoff receiving team to run back and others to run forward, thereby causing confusion, anxiety, and a disruption of the planned return. The ball will be difficult to field cleanly, especially by members of the kickoff receiving team who are typically not adept at fielding the ball and who are not expecting to have to field it. Throw in the emotion of the moment—thousands of fans yelling and teammates converging on the ball from all directions—and you have the makings of a big, momentum-shifting opportunity.

Coaching Tip: Avoid squib kicking the ball down the middle of the field in order to increase the chances that the ball will be recovered by the kicking team, that the kickoff team's planned return will be ruined, or that the ball will go out-of-bounds if mis-hit.

When to Attempt a Squib Kick

- You are kicking to a good kick-returner and/or kick-returning team.
- You are using an ineffective kickoff team or kickoff specialist.
- It is raining and the field is sloppy and slick.

How to Execute

Mark off the approach for a deep kick, and then add six to eight inches more so the ball will be struck above the sweet spot. Since it is not necessary to generate height or distance, the squib kick can be kicked using a kickoff tee or off the ground (lying sideways). Placekickers use the tee because squib kicks can be kicked more consistently from a tee and because the kickoff receiving team is not tipped off to what the kickoff team is attempting. If the ball is kicked off the ground, the kicker should shorten his approach to accommodate the fact that the ball is much lower than it would be if it were being kicked off a tee.

Coaching Tip: When deciding whether or not to use a kickoff tee, remember that the kick should be disguised as much as possible; it should not be readily apparent to the kick-receiving team that an unconventional kick of any kind is being attempted.

Straight-on Kicker

Angle the approach away from the direction the kick is intended to travel, then kick the ball as if it is being kicked deep.

Soccer-Style Kicker

Adjust the angle of the approach to kick the ball to one side of the field, then kick the ball as if it is being kicked deep.

A coach should consider all the kickoff options available to him before automatically making a decision to kick the ball deep.

Pooch Kicks

Executed properly, the pooch kick will travel in the air 20 to 30 yards downfield in a high arc with plenty of backspin. Typically, the ball will drop in between the lines of the kickoff receiving team, forcing some of the kickoff receiving team to run back and others to run forward, causing confusion, anxiety, and a disruption of the planned return.

Coaching Tip: Avoid pooch-kicking the ball down the middle of the field in order to increase the chances that the ball will be recovered by the kicking team, that the kickoff team's planned return will be ruined, or that the ball will go out-of-bounds if mishit.

When to Attempt a Pooch Kick

- You are kicking to a good kick-returner and/or a good kick-returning team.
- You are using an ineffective kickoff team or kickoff specialist.
- It is raining and the field is sloppy and slick.
- You want to get the ball back for your offense and avoid giving up good field position if the kick is unsuccessful.

How to Execute

The kickoff specialist should approach the ball exactly as he would for a regular kickoff. He should not try to kick the ball higher or shorter, and he should not take stutter steps. The only thing he should do differently is to cheat six to eight inches closer to the ball than he normally would before starting his approach. By doing so, he will end up too close to the ball at impact and his kicking foot will strike the ball well below the sweet spot, thus generating additional height and less distance.

Straight-on Kicker

While it is obviously impossible for a straight-on kicker to disguise his intent to kick the ball at an angle, that does not mean that the kickoff receiving team has to know that he is attempting a pooch kick. Angle the approach away from the direction the kick is intended to travel, and then approach and kick the ball as if it is being kicked deep.

Soccer-Style Kicker

An experienced soccer-style kicker will either decrease or increase the angle of his approach to kick the ball to one side of the field or the other, then approach and kick the ball as if it is being kicked deep.

Onside Kicks

When executed properly, the conventional onside kick will travel on the ground 10 to 12 yards downfield, bouncing hard and low, once, twice, and then popping up high on the third bounce. Typically, the ball will either drop behind the front line of the kickoff receiving team or short-hop into one of the frontline players and carom back toward the oncoming kickoff team. The onside kick is very difficult to field, especially by players who are not expecting the kick, are not the most skilled at handling the ball, and are usually starting to run downfield, away from the oncoming ball.

When to Attempt an Onside Kick

- You want to surprise the opposing team at a time when not recovering the ball will not carry unacceptable consequences. For example, you expect your defense to handle the opposing team's offense, or it is early in the game or half.
- You need to quickly get the ball back for your offense after a late score.
- It is raining and the field is sloppy and slick.

How to Execute

The kickoff team should be arrayed in one of the following formations:
- In a traditional kickoff formation spread across the field
- In a traditional formation, with the players on the field opposite the intended direction of the kick sprinting behind the other half of the formation
- With two lines arrayed one behind the other on the side of the field where the kick will be directed.

Coaching Tips: Decide on the degree to which surprise is needed; the second and third options will tip your hand unnecessarily. The kickoff specialist should approach the ball exactly as he would for a regular kickoff. He should not take stutter steps. The only things he should do differently are add six to eight inches to his approach and angle his approach such that, whether he is a straight-on or soccer-style kicker, he kicks the ball as a straight-on kicker in the desired direction. He should kick *down* on the top third of the ball, because a kicker who kicks up on the ball runs the risk of lifting the ball with a backspin that will slow the ball down. Few kickers are adept at kicking the ball off the side of their foot because it is very difficult to generate the control and erratic hops that make an onside kick so hard to handle.

The kicker's head and shoulders will be in front of the ball as the kicker bends forward and kicks down into the top third of the ball. The trouble many kickers have with this method of kicking an onside kick is that they tend to want to lean back as they would when kicking normally. However, when they lean back, they are prone to kicking the bottom third of the ball and getting a hard, end-over-end kick that clears the front line of the kickoff receiving team and goes out-of-bounds. Depending on how far from the ball they are at set-up, they may kick about midway up the ball, resulting in a hard knuckler that is very difficult for either team to get before going out-of-bounds. The other major problem that a kicker unfamiliar with this technique has is the tendency to make up for the greater distance from the ball (the additional six to eight inches) by taking longer strides when approaching the ball and/or taking stutter steps. As with the pooch and squib kicks, he must learn to trust his steps and approach the ball no differently than he would a regular kick. Such skill only comes from a great deal of practice.

Line Drive

When executed properly, the line-drive kick will knuckle through the air directly at one of the closest front-line members of the kickoff receiving team. The ball will either carom off the player back to the kickoff team or will slice through the front line, throwing the first two lines of the kickoff team in disarray as they try to catch up to a ball that is bouncing wildly downfield.

When to Attempt a Line-Drive Kick

- You want to surprise the opposing team at a time when not recovering the kick will not carry unacceptable consequences. For example, you expect your defense to handle the opposing team's offense or it is early in the game or half.
- You need to quickly get ball the back for your offense after a late score.
- It is raining and the field is sloppy and slick.

The kickoff specialist should approach the ball exactly as he would a regular kickoff. He should not take stutter steps. The only things he should do differently is to add six to eight inches to his approach and to punch—rather than kick—the ball as hard as possible. The object is to send the ball on a hard-line drive three feet off the ground without spiraling or spinning end-over-end.

8

The Mental Side of Kicking

What is the most important aspect of placekicking? What should a placekicker do to give himself the best chance to succeed? The expected answers to these questions might be something like "practice more," "work on your steps," or "kick through the ball." All of these answers are important, but none of them are the most important. What then is the most important aspect of placekicking? Quite simply, it is the most important aspect of *any* sport, yet one that is very much unappreciated and misunderstood: visualization, preparing the player's mind to succeed. Practice is important, as is watching experts compete. But neither is as important as visualizing what one needs to do and visualizing oneself doing exactly that.

A study conducted some years back illustrates the power of visualization. Researchers divided a group of basketball players into two groups of equally talented free-throw shooters. One group was directed to shoot free throws for a set time over a set number of days. The members of the second group were directed to spend the same time independently visualizing shooting free throws. At the end of the study period, both groups' free-throw shooting performance improved significantly, yet there was no statistically significant difference between the two groups' performance after the study was over. Practice makes perfect, but so does visualization. Imagine the improvement that would have been gained by combining free-throw shooting practice and visualization.

How can a serious placekicker tap into the technique's power? By sequestering himself in a quiet place for at least 15 minutes at a time as often as possible and visualizing, over and over again, the perfect measurements, the perfect balanced setup, a clean, smooth snap and hold, a perfect approach and follow-through, the feel of the kicking foot's perfect contact with the ball, and a kick that sails end-over-end, unobstructed, and up and up until it passes right down the middle of the goalposts. Every time. From every angle, especially the angle with which he has the most trouble. From every distance, within reason, of course, since the subconscious mind will not attach legitimacy to an "attempt" beyond the kicker's capabilities.

The most important aspect of *any* sport, yet one that is very much unappreciated and misunderstood: visualization, preparing the player's mind to succeed.

Whenever possible, take the kicker off to the side before every kick, even extra points. The objective is to get him to relax, focus on the task at hand (especially if he is a regular player on offense), and go on to the field with the confidence and self-assurance he will need to kick effectively. Have him close his eyes and take a deep breath. Then, talk him slowly through the kicking process: lining up the tee properly, marking off his steps properly, emphasizing the angle if that is his weakness (especially on longer kicks), the snap, the hold, his first drive step, opening his hips, and kicking up and through the ball, then watching it soar up, up, and through the goalposts. Say all of this in a positive manner, exclaiming about how well each aspect is executed to settle his nerves and enable him to focus solely on kicking the ball. If he is on the other side of the field when the team is getting ready to kick a field goal after participating in a third down play, point to your head to signal that he is to go through the preparatory routine by himself. Think of this, or a similar routine, not as a crutch but as an opportunity to help your kicker visualize success. Just as you never want your snapper, holder, or kicker to take kicking field goals for granted, do not take these routines for granted, even if (maybe especially when) the kicking game is going well. Overconfidence and neglect lead to the same negative results.

Visualization practices need not be limited to placekickers. The kickoff specialist, the snapper, and the holder can all benefit from visualizing themselves doing their respective jobs perfectly over and over again under all conditions. When practiced repeatedly, visualization will lead to greater confidence. Its greatest benefits are in preparing the mind to succeed, creating the right environment for success, and reinforcing the muscle memory that a kicker develops through the physical part of placekicking practices. To the extent that visualization reduces the placekicker's need to concentrate on all the details involved in placekicking, his performance will improve. He will, in essence, have developed into a placekicker who expects to kick well and to kick naturally, not simply as a result of going through a long list of mechanics.

9

Equipment

Even the best placekickers can be hampered by poor equipment, or at least fooled into believing they are better than they truly are (see the subsection entitled "Ball"). If you are a coach, make sure your placekickers have the proper equipment. It need not be top of the line or the highest priced, but it should be of a quality sufficient to make your placekickers comfortable and free of concern when doing their job.

Shoes

Three basic rules apply when evaluating placekickers' shoes. They must be comfortable, yet sturdy. They must be properly fitted, preferably a half size smaller than normal so that they provide a snug fit with no space between the foot and the shoe. Too much space between the toe and the shoe will reduce the amount of power and momentum that is transferred from the kicking foot to the football. The shoe on the kicking foot must not have long cleats that will drag along the turf during the kick.

Straight-on Kicker

Most people who are knowledgeable about football are familiar with the square-toed football shoe that straight-on kickers use when placekicking. The hard, flat toe provides a much more consistent and firm surface with which to make contact with the football than the typical cleat with its rounded toe. While athletic shoe retailers do not stock these specialty shoes as commonly as they used to, given that fewer and fewer placekickers use the straight-on placekicking approach, a serious straight-on kicker should be able to buy a pair without too much trouble. The high-topped, straight-on kicking shoes provide more stability and also help the placekicker keep his ankle locked during the kick. Of course, a placekicker using a regular shoe can achieve the same effect by looping a string from the cleat at the tip of the shoe around the ankle (see Figures 9-1 and 9-2). The string keeps the toe up and in place, allowing the placekicker to concentrate on kicking the ball rather than keeping his ankle cocked.

Figure 9-1

Figure 9-2

Soccer-Style Kicker

One need not be too particular when it comes to soccer-style kicking shoes. No special soccer-style placekicking shoe is truly required. Any non-high-top shoe used by soccer players, or an all-purpose athletic shoe with cleats, will suffice as long as the leather provides a snug fit along the length and width of the foot, and the cleat base does not protrude from the sides of the foot.

Ball

Most coaches allow their placekickers to use only the more worn-out footballs, understandably saving the best balls for their quarterbacks. Placekickers do not need to practice with the best footballs and, if they did, the footballs would wear out much sooner. However, it must be recognized that a coach who gives his placekickers only the worst footballs with which to practice runs at least two risks: first, purposely or otherwise, publicly devaluing or denigrating his placekickers, and second, improperly preparing his placekickers for game conditions. Given that many people—including a placekicker's own teammates—already undervalue the placekicker, the former should be a major concern.

To appreciate why the latter should be a concern, compare the current week's game ball to the last week's game ball (used during the most recent week of practice). With only one week's worth of use by quarterbacks, receivers, and running backs, the previous week's game ball is already both slightly larger and more elastic. Now compare them with the best and worst balls that the placekicker uses during his practices. The size and elasticity of the kicking practice balls are typically much greater than a one-week-old game ball, much less the current week's game ball.

What effect will the size and elasticity differences have on a placekicker's efforts? Often, a very dramatic effect. First, the extent to which a practice ball is larger than a game ball will determine the degree to which a placekicker's steps will be off during a game and the higher the ball will be struck when kicked. Thus, the placekicker will lose height, accuracy, and, if the contact point is too high, distance. Second, the harder, less resilient game ball will not travel as far, or as high, as a practice ball. Thus, to the extent that a practice ball is more elastic than a game ball, his and your expectations of his kicking prowess will be "inflated." During the 1970s, for example, placekickers in some football college conferences were allowed to bring a regulation ball of their choosing into a game solely for their field-goal attempts and kickoffs without making one of the balls part of the game-ball rotation. The result was longer field goals.

Kickoff Tee

It is truly amazing how much kicking tees have evolved over the years. After all, what was there to change about the "lowly" kickoff tee? A lot, actually, given the growing popularity and use of soccer-style kicking. The old-style kickoff tee is perfect for a straight-on kicker. It holds the ball up straight, allows the kicker to tilt the ball as much as he wants or needs to, has no protrusions that interfere with the kicker's motion up and through the ball, and can be used by either a right- or left-footed kicker.

However, the old-style tee (See Figure 9-3) is not ideal for a soccer-style kicker who uses a sweeping motion from the side. In fact, it is not uncommon to find one of the "arms" broken off by the constant pounding it receives from a soccer-style kicker (see Figure 9-4). Alternative tees were developed for this reason Note that the soccer-style kicking tee (Figure 9-5) has no large protrusions on one side, so there is no interference with the kicker's foot as it sweeps through the kick. The drawback, though, is that there are right-footed and left-footed versions, and the kicker must buy the correct one. Of course, nothing prevents a kicker from modifying the old-style tee by purposely lopping off the interfering "arm," as in Figure 9-4. Doing so will not take away its effectiveness for straight-on kickers.

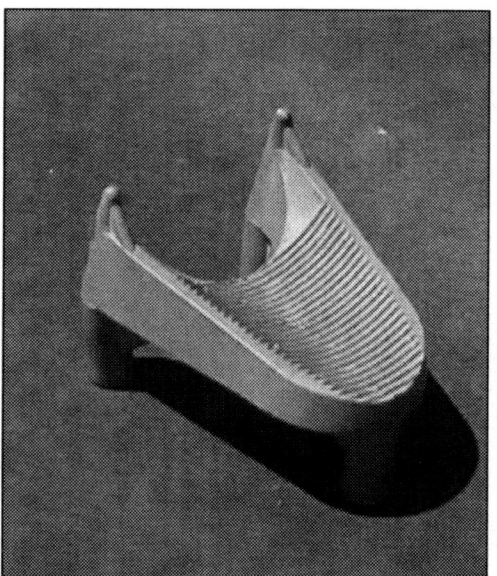

Figure 9-3

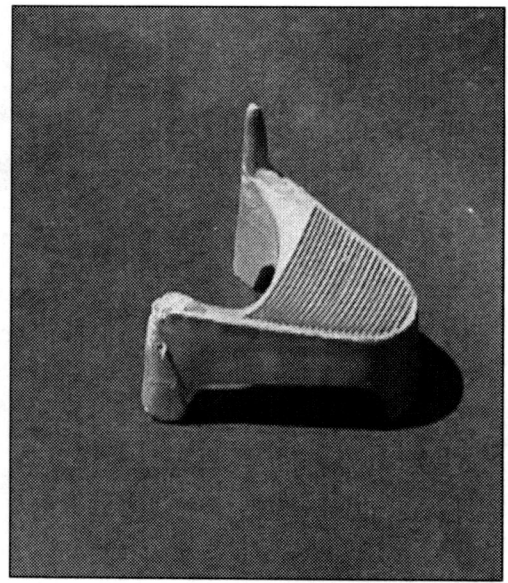

Figure 9-4

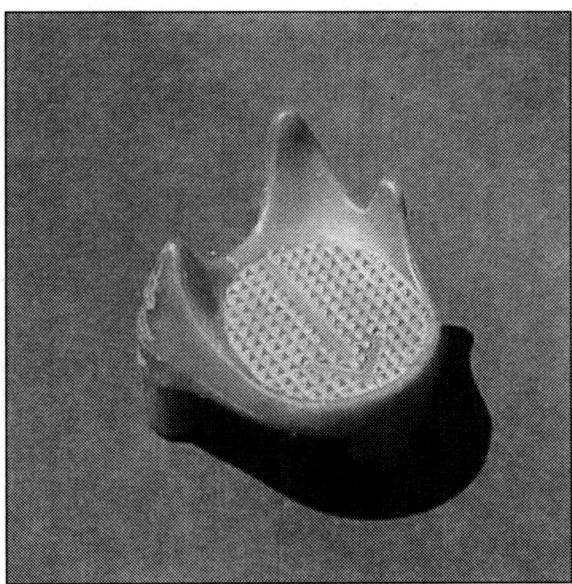
Figure 9-5

The next step in the evolution of the kickoff tee was to take away both protrusions and replace them with a depression into which the ball is placed. After all, the drawback to the soccer-style kicking tee is that it is meant for either a right- or a left-footed kicker, not both. The result is a tee, now actually a block, which can be used not only for soccer-style kickers (using either foot), but for straight-on kickers as well.

Placekicking Blocks and Tees

As was mentioned earlier, all levels below college may and do use a kicking block when attempting field goals and extra points (see Figure 9-6). Professional and college placekickers must kick the football directly off the ground. The placekicking blocks are typically two inches high, although one-inch tees are available and are increasingly being used by high school placekickers who wish to prepare themselves for college placekicking by gradually lessening their dependence on a kicking block. Note that the two ends of the block are cut at different angles. Straight-on placekickers use the sharper angle, since their kicking foot rises at a sharper angle than the foot of a soccer-style placekicker, who uses a sweeping motion when kicking.

The problem with a placekicking block is that it requires a holder to spot the ball during practices, because there is nothing to hold the ball upright. Several quite ingenious developments have arisen to remedy this situation (see Figures 9-7 through 9-11). Professional and college placekickers can use the ring in Figure 9-8, since it is sturdy enough to hold a ball by itself without the block.

Figure 9-6

Figure 9-7. Block with "arm"

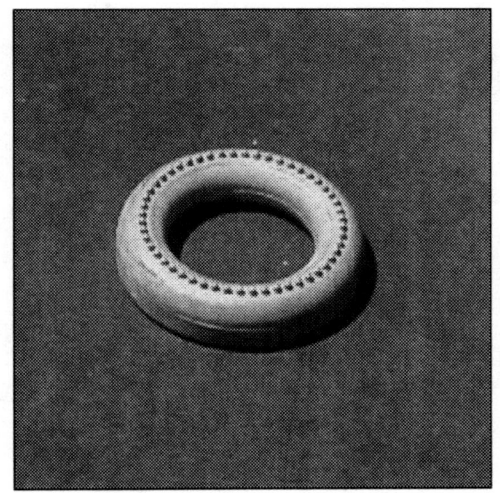

Figure 9-8. Kicking ring

Figure 9-9. Block with ring

Figure 9-10. Round block (side view)

Figure 9-11. Round block (bottom view)

10

Winning Practices, Game Preparation, and Games

Practice has no substitute, whether it is baseball, basketball, mathematics, or any other endeavor. It is no different for placekicking. If you want to be a consistent placekicker, or you want to have a consistent placekicking team that can produce whether or not the game is on the line, plenty of practice is the only way to get there.

Practice, and always supervise that practice whether it is during regular practice time, or during pre-game practices. It is always amazing, disappointing, and frustrating to see coaches leaving placekickers, holders, and snappers to their own devices during pre-game practices. How else will these three players get the coaching and encouragement they need right before crunch time? How else will you know how well they are working together, how far they can kick field goals that day or night, and what hash marks they are the most comfortable kicking from? A simple word from a coach during pre-game practices can help the kicker by aligning him properly or reminding him to follow through better, or can help the holder catch the ball more smoothly. Remember, the more the snapper, holder, and placekicker struggle individually, or as a team, during pre-game practice, the more they will lose the confidence to perform when called upon to do so during the game.

At the end of this chapter are schedules for winning practices, as well as game preparations for placekickers and coaches who are serious about this aspect of the game. Modify them to the extent that time and personnel restrict what you can and cannot do, but modify them as little as possible to give you the best chance for success.

Coaching Tips: During games, avoid kicking from the hash marks as much as possible. Remember, the shorter the field-goal kicking distance, the sharper the angle will be when kicking from the hash marks, thereby negating the advantage of a shorter field-goal attempt. Determine a hash mark from which your placekicker is more comfortable kicking.

Make sure that your placekicker and holder are ready whenever your offense appears to be headed toward field-goal-kicking opportunity. Make your holder take as many snaps as possible (insist that he practice placing the ball, not just catching it) and that your placekicker gets stretched, hops on his kicking leg to pump his leg muscles up, and begins his visualization routine. Typically, alert your holder to start taking practice snaps once the offense reaches the 40-yard line. This assumes, of course, that he is not a regular offensive player. If he is, then do what you can to get him out of the game soon enough to give him the time he needs to reacquaint himself with the art of catching and holding the ball for kicks. This works doubly well if the snapper is available; if not, either have another player help out, or simply toss the ball underhand to the holder.

Be prepared to call a time-out if you notice your placekicker is lined up improperly (especially when kicking from the hash marks), or if a delay is keeping the field-goal-kicking team from the field. Why make the snapper, holder, and placekicker rush through a difficult maneuver, thereby sacrificing one, or three, valuable points?

Coaching Tips: Know your placekicker's limitations. Adjust the distance to your kicker's ability. Do not practice kicks beyond what he can manage at least 30 percent of the time or spend time at a distance that you know you would rarely consider trying in a game (whether or not he can manage the distance).

Limit the number of extra points you attempt during practice; substitute severe-angle kicks as much as possible. Extra points are the easiest and most frequently attempted kick, requiring the least amount of form and attention to measurements and mechanics. However, severe-angle kicking (because it gives kickers so little margin for error) forces kickers to concentrate, and to get in the habit of properly measuring their steps, approaching the ball properly, and kicking with the proper follow-through.

Five-yard and Severe-angle Kicking (From Each Side)

If your placekicker plays another position, substitute up to five kicks of each for the shorter kicks listed in the practice schedules in every other practice. If your placekicker plays no other position, make sure he practices kicking on his own from the five-yard line, and from severe angles.

Daily Pre-Practice Schedule

Warm-up (5 minutes)
Stretching:
    hurdler's stretch
    lay-back
    tuck
    side-to-side
Jogging: 100 to 200 yards (while snapper and holder practice together)

Approach and follow-through (2 minutes)
Placekicker solo while snapper and holder practice together

Kicking with snapper and holder (10 minutes)
Extra points: two
Snap from hash marks between 15- and 20-yard lines: three from each side
Snap from hash marks between 25- and 30-yard lines: three from each side
Snap from 25-yard line hash marks: two from each side

Kickoffs (3 minutes)
Onside, pooch, squib, line-drive, then full

Weekly Practice Schedule

Field goal with full rush (25 minutes)
From various spots (20 minutes)
    short
    hash marks (both)
    long
Fake field-goal plays (5 minutes)
    holder bootleg
    holder sprint-out
    kicker sprint-out

Kickoff using kickoff specialist at all times (30 minutes)

Full kick, squib, pooch, line drive, and onside
Kickoff team focus (10 minutes)
Kickoff return team focus (10 minutes)
Both teams focus (10 minutes)

Leg-strengthening

If your placekicker plays another position, his practices at the other position(s) may be adequate to build strength, though additional work on his own is ideal. If your placekicker plays no other position, make sure he puts in the necessary resistance (and limited weight) training, as well as bleacher and roadwork (see Chapter 5, "Leg Flexibility and Strength") on his own during practices.

Snapper

Make sure the snapper always simulates game conditions. He cannot pick up the ball to grip it better, and he must snap it where it lies; so set it between, for example, the 32- and 33-yard lines rather than right on either line.

Spotting the Ball

Simulating game conditions for the snapper will force your kicker and holder to simulate game conditions as well, for example, making sure the ball is spotted seven yards from where it is snapped, regardless of where it is snapped.

Visualization

Make sure your placekicker, snapper, and holder all understand the value of visualization techniques. Moderate for them at first so they can see your dedication to, and belief in, this facet of training. Make it a habit to chart your kickers' practice kicks so that you and they understand their strengths and weaknesses. Spend some time during pre-game practices attempting the kicks that your kickers have the most trouble with. Always end on a successful kick, even if that means kicking short, straight-away field goals, so that your snapper, holder, and kicker walk away on a high note, because they will carry that feeling into the first attempt they are called upon to make. It is even advisable to roundly praise a failed last pre-game practice attempt, emphasizing what the players did well or giving them a legitimate excuse like the wind, the heaviness of the ball, and so forth, for missing the kick. In other words, give them something positive that they can latch on to that will take away the sting of a missed attempt so that they enter the game with a positive mindset.

Make sure your kickers bear down during practices. It is awfully easy for them to get frustrated, bored, or disinterested during kicking practice, especially if they are doing very well or very poorly. Novice soccer-style kickers, especially those with a soccer playing background, are most often the kickers who need to bear down the most since they do not yet understand the complexity involved in kicking consistently. They often still think of placekicking as just winding up and kicking the ball, something they think any decent soccer player can do with little effort. You can see it in their approach and follow-through; neither is done with much conviction and, consequently, their kicking results are inconsistent.

Your major objective as a placekicking coach should be to treat your kickers as students who must be taught the whys and wherefores of placekicking so well that they do not need you anymore, can correct their own mistakes, can make the necessary adjustments, and can go through the visualization techniques. They should learn to know from the feel of the approach into the kick, and the feel and sound of the foot making contact with the ball, whether or not they have kicked the ball properly.

Pre-Game Schedule

Warm-up (5 minutes)
Running across the field and back, while snapper and holder practice together
Stretching:
    hurdler's stretch
    lay-back
    tuck
    side-to-side

Approach and follow-through (2 minutes)
Placekicker only while snapper and holder practice together

Kicking with snapper and holder (10 minutes)
Extra points: four
30 to 35-yard-line hash marks: four from each side
40-yard-line hash marks: two from each side
45-yard-line hash marks: one or two from each side

Kickoffs (3 minutes)
Full only

Game Schedule

- Stretching, jogging in place.

- Kicking into a net.

- Priming the muscles. Hopping in place with both legs, then just the kicking leg, to keep the kicking muscles warm and pumped up. Players should not do too much, or the leg will tire. Placekickers should prime the muscles when your team's offense gets into field-goal range.

- Practicing visualization techniques.

Epilogue

I have tried to clearly and concisely capture my years of kicking experience into this book, and, for the most part, I feel I have succeeded. I truly love the art and science of placekicking, and I love passing on my knowledge to young athletes and coaches who are truly interested in developing a solid and consistent kicking program. I am an analytical person by nature, and I had to rely on that analytic bent when I was just starting out in the sport. I had to dissect my own placekicking mechanics and results, and figure out just why I would kick the ball well one time but not another. I never had a placekicking coach who truly understood how to placekick, but that ultimately worked to my benefit because now I have the detailed knowledge and understanding to pass along placekicking skills to others.

I know I have gone into quite a lot of detail regarding the kicking game in general and the fundamental mechanics of placekicking. I hope not so much that your head is swimming and you are having trouble assimilating it all. If so, my advice is to go back to the beginning of the book and highlight those sections that make the most sense to you and that you feel you can readily explain to your placekickers.

Bear in mind that if you are having trouble assimilating all the advice, your placekickers will as well. Go slowly, become comfortable with the basics, closely watch your kickers' mechanics, and correct the most glaring deficiencies. Do not try to change everything at once. Find a way to ensure that your placekickers improve, if only marginally.

I wish you and your placekickers nothing but the best!

About the Author

Steve Libassi earned William & Mary's first placekicking scholarship and went on to set or tie several of the school's placekicking records during his four-year career. Steve has over 30 years of experience as a placekicker and as a placekicking coach at the college, high school, and recreation-league levels. He is the holder of a patent for an athletic shoe design that ensures longer wear and a smoother surface for soccer and placekicking. He lives in Roanoke, VA, with his wife, Mary Sue, and two sons, Nathan and Collin.